# yOung
# Exceptional
# children

## Monograph Series No. 12

# Supporting Young Children with Autism Spectrum Disorders and Their Families

## THE DIVISION FOR EARLY CHILDHOOD
## OF THE COUNCIL FOR EXCEPTIONAL CHILDREN

**Hannah H. Schertz, Connie Wong, and Samuel L. Odom**
*Co-Editors*

## Disclaimer

The opinions and information contained in the articles in this publication are those of the authors of the respective articles and not necessarily those of the co-editors of the *Young Exceptional Children (YEC)* Monograph Series or of the Division for Early Childhood. Accordingly, the Division for Early Childhood assumes no liability or risk that may be incurred as a consequence, directly or indirectly, or the use and application of any of the contents of this publication.

The DEC does not perform due diligence on advertisers, exhibitors, or their products or services, and cannot endorse or guarantee that their offerings are suitable or accurate.

ISSN 1096-2506 • ISBN 978-0-9819327-4-3

Printed in the United States of America

Published and Distributed by:

27 Fort Missoula Road, Suite 2
Missoula, MT 59804
(406) 543-0872
FAX (406) 543-0887
www.dec-sped.org

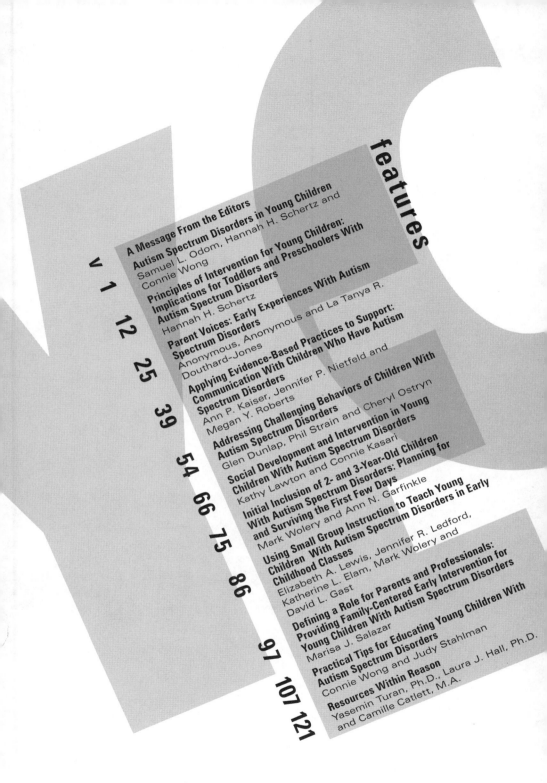

features

# A Message From the Editors

Welcome to the 12th issue of the *Young Exceptional Children* Monograph Series. This volume is designed to provide practical guidance for work with young children who have autism spectrum disorders (ASD) and their families. Our editorial team wanted the monograph to provide meaningful solutions to everyday issues of concern to service providers. We began our planning for this issue by identifying topics related to the most pervasive challenges experienced by toddlers and preschoolers with ASD—social, communication, and behavioral—then extended our reach to topics with universal relevance (i.e., useful in work with all children with ASD rather than a subset of children). Many more manuscript submissions were received than could be accepted within our space limitations including those on topics of play, integrated community supports, music therapy, collaborating with families through electronic communication, feeding strategies, and specific "branded" approaches to intervention. Watch for some of these articles in forthcoming *Young Exceptional Children* journal issues.

In the introductory chapter, Odom and colleagues describe the landscape of ASD historically and currently. Descriptions of increasing prevalence rates and the wide range in characteristics and outcomes for children with ASD have important implications for intervention planning at the individual and system levels. Readers will find a timely summary of the revised diagnostic criteria for ASD that were released recently in draft form. The sections on early signs of ASD, screening resources, and characteristics of high-quality diagnostic evaluation are essential reading for those in contact with young children who are not yet identified but who have early signs of ASD. Early identification is vital to ensure access to appropriate services during the toddler years when critical social-communication foundations are established. The chapter also addresses questions often asked of early intervention and early childhood special education professionals, such as "Why is there an increase in prevalence?" and "Do vaccines cause ASD?" Web-based links point readers to further resources in areas of particular interest.

In addition to ASD-specific considerations, recommendations of the Division for Early Childhood of the Council for Exceptional Children (DEC; Sandall, Hemmeter, Smith, & McLean, 2005) framed the monograph. In chapter 2, Schertz reviews broad principles of practice for young children, including those recommended by DEC. Focused on five areas, the principles call for intervention that is family-centered and strengths-based, implemented through natural and inclusive environments, grounded in developmental foundations of social communication, coordinated and systematic, and oriented toward functional and active learning. Implications for ASD are addressed for each principle. This chapter reminds professionals that children and families are not defined solely by ASD, but that holistic principles of good practice apply.

Douthard-Jones and two parents writing anonymously set the stage for the chapters that follow by painting a vivid picture of the impact of having children with ASD on themselves and their family systems. Common threads emerge from their diverse experiences. Early themes center on parents' initial experiences with ASD, including recognizing early signs, waiting for answers, and introspective thoughts. Other themes concern challenges in navigating the service system and disparate priorities or interests that sometimes emerged among families, professionals, and children. Finally, all three parents addressed the role of hope and empowerment in the process of coming to terms with their children's ASD. This has important implications for how practitioners support families during early periods of crisis. Although it is important to paint a realistic picture, professionals' emphasis on children's and families' strengths and potential rather than deficits, impairments, and limitations can play a critical role in enhancing family well-being.

The next three chapters focus on the triad of social, communication, and behavioral challenges for children with ASD. Kaiser and her colleagues describe essential components of a comprehensive approach to social communication intervention, illustrating specific strategies to address each component. They emphasize that to be functional and meaningful, communication intervention cannot be divorced from its social context. This has implications for supporting the parent-child relationship as a natural medium for communication learning. Nonverbal engagement is promoted as a foundation for communication intervention, showing that the social and communication aspects of intervention are interconnected. Additional components focus on creating ample opportunities for communication and employing naturalistic and systematic strategies to fine-tune communication skills toward greater complexity. Readers will find that this chapter is closely linked to recommended practices and sound research.

Dunlap, Strain, and Ostryn introduce a multilevel approach to intervention that follows a response-to-intervention framework for addressing behavioral challenges. Overlaying their specific recommendations is a call to address challenging behaviors in the context of the whole child and to view families as important intervention partners. The authors stress the importance of the social context for interventions in that learning to interact appropriately is most successful when it occurs from within natural social interactions and is linked to establishing friendships. Finally, the authors emphasize that because children show challenging behaviors for individually specific reasons, indirect means such as arranging the environmental and promoting alternative skills are powerful strategies for promoting more productive behavior.

Lawton and Kasari describe early social concerns in ASD with a special focus on joint attention and symbolic play. Both are important for later development of verbal social communication. Joint attention is a pre-verbal form of sharing attention with another person and an important precursor of language. Also, because language is a symbolic form of communication, symbolic play serves a foundational role as well. This chapter is a must-read for early interventionists who need guidance on how to focus intervention goals for preverbal toddlers with ASD.

The following four chapters operationalize some of the principles introduced in chapter 2. Wolery and Garfinkle focus on steps preschool personnel can take to ensure that the important first few days of inclusive classroom placements are a success. Their useful recommendations address pre-enrollment preparation, easing family concerns about the child's adjustment and separation, preparing for classroom transitions, and recognizing and managing initial behavioral challenges. This chapter is essential reading for teachers who work in inclusive early childhood settings or those exploring ways to make such arrangements for young children with ASD a reality.

In chapter 8, Lewis and her colleagues introduce a persuasive rationale and a practical framework for promoting learning within small groups, an important alternative or supplement to individualized one-to-one formats. Preschool teachers need feasible solutions to the challenge of accommodating individual learning goals within group settings. The framework offered here explores methods for diversifying small-group instruction, making learning engaging, and setting expectations through a comfortable and predictable structure.

Salazar follows with a rationale and strategies for a naturalistic, behaviorally oriented approach that directly involves families in intervention delivery. These strategies are grounded in an embedded instruction framework that emphasizes contextual support, environmental arrangement, and specific behavioral strategies such as time delay,modeling, prompting and fading, and natural reinforcement.

In the final chapter, Wong and Stahlman pull the monograph together with tips related to assessment, individual planning, systematic instruction, and engagement with families and teams. They return frequently to a real-world case scenario, illustrating how interventionists might address specific predicaments, such as targeting what is meaningful and important for a young child with ASD to learn, identifying resources for evidence-based practices, keeping track of child progress, and working with families and across disciplines. Through their case story approach, the authors help the reader escape narrow or simplistic solutions for problems that they may confront in practice.

The final piece in this 12th Monograph is an article entitled "Resources within Reason." Yasmin Turan and Camille Catlett have partnered to provide you with information about low-cost but high-quality resources for materials to support your efforts in serving young children with autism and their families. This feature is very similar to those you will find in each issue of *Young Exceptional Children*.

Readers will discover common threads among the 10 chapters of the monograph, revealing important interrelationships. For example, in chapter 5 we see that communication is closely linked with early social interaction and also has an important role in preventing and addressing challenging behavior. The social context is emphasized in several chapters, as is establishing joint attention as a foundation for social communication. These recurring themes show that good intervention is an integrated process—that areas of intervention are interconnected and that the whole child and family are our chief concerns. We hope the monograph will inspire readers to continue exploring recommended practices for young children with ASD in *Young Exceptional Children* and other sources.

The editorial team extends warm appreciation first to Carla Peterson for her helpful support and practical assistance. We also thank each of the contributors for their insights, their contributions to the field through this and other efforts, and their flexibility to align their manuscripts with the monograph's intended purpose.

**Reference**

Sandall, S. R., Hemmeter, M. L., Smith, B. J., & McLean, M. E. (2005). *DEC recommended practices: A comprehensive guide for practical application in early intervention/early childhood special education.* Missoula, MT: Division for Early Childhood (DEC), Council for Exceptional Children.

Co-Editors:    Hannah H. Schertz    (hschertz@indiana.edu)
               Connie Wong           (connie.wong@unc.edu)
               Samuel L. Odom        (slodom@unc.edu)

# Autism Spectrum Disorders in Young Children

**Samuel L. Odom, Ph.D.,**
FPG Child Development Institute, University of North Carolina, Chapel Hill

**Hannah H. Schertz, Ph.D.,**
Indiana University, Bloomington

**Connie Wong, Ph.D.,**
FPG Child Development Institute, University of North Carolina, Chapel Hill

**T**wo boys with autism spectrum disorders (ASD) attended an inclusive preschool class in a small, rural community. The teachers had to keep a close eye on Jesse due to his tendency to eat foods or edible-looking objects that were left unguarded. Jesse rarely looked people in the eye, preferring to focus on solitary activities of his own choosing. He occasionally flapped his hands and made noises, although he rarely spoke words and never used them to communicate. Jesse did not play with other children and moved away when peers attempted to be friendly. However, it was clear that he was aware of his peers because in a crowded room with children on the floor, he would skillfully step around outstretched arms or legs, whereas he did not hesitate to occasionally step up on furniture, blocks, or other objects. Norman, in contrast, was a very verbal child who spoke in sentences, although not always with relevance to the topic at hand. He was quite attached to classroom routines and would voice concern (sometimes with tantrums) about changes in the routine. During center time, Norman played only with toy rocket ships and dinosaurs and strongly resisted others' attempts to shift his interest to other activities. Once when Norman said he went to a movie about dinosaurs and the teacher asked what it was about, he described the entire sequence of scenes in the movie.

Autism spectrum disorders (ASD) span a great range of ability levels and potential life trajectories. This presents challenges for teachers, family members, and others who seek to understand the commonalities and differences among young children with ASD and to put this knowledge to use in intervention planning. Over the past 25 years, ASD has changed from a low-prevalence disorder to one seen frequently in early childhood programs. Because certain teaching and intervention practices appear to have great potential for promoting positive outcomes for young children with ASD and their families (National Research Council, 2001; Odom, Rogers, McDougle, Hume, & McGee, 2007), early interventionists and early childhood special educators play a critical role in first identifying young children with ASD as well as planning and providing early intervention/early childhood special education services.

The purpose of this chapter is to provide an overview of ASD and its identification early in the lives of children and families. This introductory information is important because (1) diagnostic criteria for ASD is in the process of changing, (2) unsubstantiated claims (myths) about the cause of ASD exist and have repercussions for the rest of society, and (3) early childhood professionals are a critical link in the processes of early identification and intervention. We begin by describing the characteristics of ASD and follow with descriptions of the history of the disorder, "red flags" that suggest the need for evaluation, screening tools, and diagnostic criteria.

## ASD: The Definition

ASD is an "unofficial" term used to group several psychiatrically defined diagnoses that fall along a range or spectrum of characteristics. In the fourth edition of the *Diagnostic and Statistical Manual of Mental Disorders (DSM-IV-TR*; American Psychological Association [APA], 2000), the most commonly used guide for diagnosis of ASD in the United States, autistic disorder is the most often diagnosed of the spectrum, but three other disorders share similar characteristics: Asperger's disorder, Rett's disorder, Childhood Disintegrative Disorder, and Pervasive Developmental Disorder Not Otherwise Specified (PDD-NOS). These diagnoses are all grouped under the larger category of Pervasive Developmental Disorders (PDD). PDD has become synonymous with the term ASD, because all of these disorders share common characteristics that fall along a spectrum or continuum.

Autistic disorder is the diagnostic classification closest to the disorder that Kanner first identified as autism in the 1940s (Kanner, 1943). Three broad sets of characteristics define autistic disorder: (1) difficulty engaging in social interactions and/or establishing social relationships; (2) delayed, nonexistent, or disordered (i.e., echolalia) use of language to communicate; and (3) restricted repetitive stereotypic behavior, such

Table 1

| Current classification: Pervasive Developmental Disorder | Proposed changes: Autism Spectrum Disorder (ASD) |
|---|---|
| • Autistic disorder<br>• Asperger's syndrome<br>• Child disintegrative disorder<br>• Rett's syndrome<br>• Pervasive developmental disorder not otherwise specified (PDD-NOS) | • Most severe ASD<br>• Moderately severe ASD<br>• Less severe ASD<br>• Subclinical ASD symptoms |

as moving hands in repeated or unusual patterns, rocking, or "special interests." First signs of these symptoms appear before age 36 months. For a minority of children with autistic disorder, normal development occurs for a period of time, and then they regress (e.g., stop using words to communicate, become less social) and begin showing the symptoms just noted.

The other disorders grouped within ASD share some of the characteristics of autistic disorder (see Table 1). At different ages and levels of severity, characteristics of autism are manifested in different ways. For example, for Jesse social interaction and communication were largely absent and he clearly displayed stereotypic behavior. Norman communicated in most ways we would expect for a boy his age, but his communication was not always socially appropriate and his special interests often dominated his communication.

At the time of this writing, the APA was considering a revision of the *DSM-IV-TR* criteria, which will appear as the fifth edition (see Swedo [2010] and http://www.dsm5.org). They propose to replace the current set of PDD diagnostic categories with a single classification called Autism Spectrum Disorder. Also, APA proposes to revise the diagnostic indicators from the current three to two: (1) impairments in social communication abilities and (2) occurrence of fixed interest and repetitive behavior. In addition, it proposes a continuum of severity to include "most severe ASD," "moderately severe ASD," "less severe ASD," and "subclinical ASD symptoms." Descriptions of how those forms of ASD are manifest at different ages would be provided in the new classification system. It is important to note that these changes have not yet taken effect as of this writing and may change following input from the field.

*APA proposes to revise the diagnostic indicators from the current three to two: impairments in social communication abilities and occurrence of fixed interest and repetitive behavior.*

## Facts About ASD

ASD affect boys about four to five times as often as girls (Autism Interaction Network, 2010; http://www.iancommunity.org/cs/ian_research_reports/ian_research_report_dec_2009). The prevalence rates have changed over the years, with the most current rate reported by the Centers for Disease Control and Prevention (CDC) being 1 in 70 for boys, 1 in 315 in girls, with an overall prevalence rate of 1 in 110 (CDC, 2009). This may be compared with prevalence rates of 2 to 5 per 10,000 reported in the 1980s (Zahner & Pauls, 1987). Although ASD occurs across socioeconomic and ethnic groups, children from African American and Latino families are diagnosed less frequently than children from nonminority groups or groups less affected by high poverty rates (Mandell et al., 2009). At one time, intellectual disability was thought to be a co-occurring condition for at least 75% of children with autistic disorder; however, with the inclusion of the broader spectrum of ASD and more accurate assessment approaches for individuals with ASD, the co-occurrence of intellectual disability in the ASD population is likely to be lower than once suspected (Hyman & Towbin, 2007).

### Why Is There an Increase in Prevalence?

Professionals are often asked whether more children have ASD today than they did 25 years ago, and if so, why? Epidemiologists who study prevalence think that there has not been a true increase in the condition (Fombonne, 2009), but with the broadening of the diagnostic criteria in the *DSM-IV-TR* to include a spectrum of disorders, more individuals are included under the ASD umbrella. Also, it is possible that there has been a diagnostic shift, with some children originally classified as having intellectual disability now being classified as having ASD. For example, Jesse fits the more classic autistic disorder profile, although in a previous era he might have instead been classified as having severe mental retardation. Norman does not fit the classic autistic disorder profile and may have gone undiagnosed, simply being considered an odd and difficult child rather than one who has ASD. In addition, there is greater public awareness, better and earlier screening approaches, and better diagnostic assessment tools, all of which may influence prevalence rates.

### What Causes ASD?

**Influence of Genetics**. Once thought to be a disorder caused by poor child rearing, there is common agreement now that ASD is a neurodevelopmental disorder with genetic origins. Some genetic syndromes are associated with ASD, such as Rett's syndrome, Fragile X

*ASD is a neurodevelopmental disorder with genetic origins.*

syndrome, and tuberous sclerosis, but for the majority of children with ASD, links to a specific genetic syndrome have not been found. Yet, even though an exact genetic link has not been discovered, results of twin and sibling studies suggest a strong genetic association with the occurrence of ASD (Dawson, 2008; Landa & Garrett-Mayer, 2006).

**Do Vaccines Cause ASD?** One of the most controversial and emotional topics related to ASD, and one that has far-reaching public health implications, is whether vaccines for common childhood illnesses cause the onset of ASD. Influenced by parents who have reported that their children first began showing symptoms of ASD soon after they were vaccinated, this movement has become a cause célèbre for some public figures. The larger public health implication is that some parents have not had their children vaccinated due to the parents' fear that it will trigger the onset of ASD; this has resulted in increases in diseases such as measles that were one thought to be eradicated. Some deaths have even been reported from these resurgent diseases. However, numerous systematic studies have shown no relationship between the incidence of ASD and immunization (Parker, Schwartz,

*Numerous systematic studies have shown no relationship between the incidence of ASD and immunization.*

Todd, & Pickering, 2004), and recently the initial article claiming vaccines as a cause of pervasive developmental disorders (Wakefield et al., 1998) was refuted by editors of *The Lancet* (2010), which is the prestigious medical journal that originally published the paper.

## Brief History of ASD and Services in the United States

The identification of autism originated in the psychiatric clinic of Leo Kanner (Kanner, 1943), when he identified a group of children, mostly boys, who exhibited similar characteristics. Coincidentally, at nearly the same time in Vienna, Hans Asperger (1944/1991) began writing about children and youth with similar characteristics, although this information was not available in the United States until well after World War II. Early treatments for children with autism were influenced by the psychoanalytic theory of the times, as reflected by Bruno Bettelheim (1967), which proposed that inadequate caregiving provided by "refrigerator mothers" caused the autism in their children. In subsequent years, this approach was debunked and alternative approaches emerged in the structured teaching approach developed by Schopler, Brehm, Kinsbourne, and Reichler (1971), which became the TEACCH program, and in the applied behavioral analysis approach designed by Ivar Lovaas (Lovaas, 1971; Lovaas Institute, 2010). From these early beginnings, a range of comprehensive service models (Odom, Boyd, Hall, & Hume, 2010) and focused intervention practices (National Autism Center, 2009; Odom, Colett-Klingenberg, Rogers, & Hatton, in press) have emerged. In 1992, autism was included as an eligibility category for special education services in the Individuals With Disabilities Education Act. For children younger than 36 months, autism or ASD is not currently designated specifically as an eligibility category for early intervention (Part C) services in many states, but infants and toddlers diagnosed as having ASD are usually eligible for services under other state-designed classifications such as developmental delay (Boyd, Odom, Humphreys, & Sam, in press).

## Identifying Autism Early

Although intervention and appropriate treatment at any age is important, there is some evidence that intervening earlier may have powerful effects for children with ASD (National Research Council, 2001). However, parents providing information to the Interactive Autism Network (2010) reported substantial delays in their children receiving a diagnosis of ASD after their first expression of concern about their children's development, with the age of diagnosis (and time between first concern and diagnosis) being 3.2 years (1.7 years delay in diagnosis) for autism, 3.7 years (2.1 years delay in diagnosis) for children with PDD-NOS, and 7.2 years (4.6 years delay) for children with Asperger's syndrome. Mandell, Novak, and Zubritsky (2005) found that diagnoses occurred even later for families in rural areas and those with lower incomes, but occurred earlier for children with more severe or visible characteristics such as absence of language or stereotypic behavior.

*Intervening earlier may have powerful effects for children with ASD. However, parents . . . report substantial delays in their children receiving a diagnosis.*

### Recognizing Early Indicators

The onset of ASD occurs, by definition, before the age of 3 years, but signs begin to appear earlier in development. These early signs are evident to watchful parents and professionals. The CDC (2010) developed a user-friendly resource with video examples (available at http://www.cdc.gov/ncbddd/actearly/concerned.html) that describes typical early milestones and how development diverges for children with ASD. The following early indicators, adapted from the CDC resources, may signal to parents, child care providers, and health care workers the need for screening.

- Not playing "pretend" games by 18 months
- Not pointing at objects to show interest by 18 months
- Not looking at objects when someone points to them
- Showing difficulty relating to others or having no interest in other people
- Avoiding eye contact and wanting to be alone
- Having trouble understanding others' feelings or talking about feelings
- Preferring not to be held or cuddled
- Appearing to be unaware when people talk to them but responding to other noises
- Having interest in people but not knowing how to relate, talk to, or play with them
- Repeating or "echoing" words or phrases said to them
- Having trouble expressing their needs with words
- Repeating actions over and over again
- Having trouble adapting when routines change
- Having unusual reactions to the way things smell, taste, look, or sound
- Losing previously acquired skills (e.g., no longer saying words used previously)

Other resources to support early identification include a video glossary created by Autism Speaks with toddler examples (searchable from http://www.autismspeaks.org) and links on the Autism Society of America Web site (http://wwwautism-society.org).

## Screening

The presence of early signs of autism calls for screening to determine whether more formal evaluation is needed. The American Academy of Neurology (Filipek et al., 2000) recommends several steps that support the process of early identification of ASD. Surveillance begins with parents and care providers being made aware of early signs and given outlets to voice their concerns. Screening should be included in all well-child checks, beginning at 18 months and using reliable screening instruments. Additional guidance on screening is available at http://www.ddhealthinfo.org (California Department of Developmental Services, 2002).

One of the most frequently used screening instruments for ASD is the Modified Checklist for Autism in Toddlers (M-CHAT; Robins, Fein, Barton, & Green, 2001), available free from http://www2.gsu.edu/~psydlr/Diana_L._Robins,_Ph.D..html. The M-CHAT is a simple checklist that caregivers complete. It is easily scored and provides reliable information about risk for ASD. Other screening instruments targeted for use in the general population include the First Year Inventory (Reznick, Baranek, Reavis, Watson, & Crais, 2007) and the Infant-Toddler Checklist (Wetherby, Brosnan-Maddox, Peace, & Newton, 2008). Both identify risk indicators that may arise by 12 months. All children identified through screening as having high risk for ASD should be referred immediately for diagnostic assessment.

*All children identified through screening as having high risk for ASD should be referred immediately for diagnostic assessment.*

## Diagnosis

Diagnosis of ASD in children as young as age 2, when made by trained professionals, is now considered to be reliable and stable (Lord et al., 2006). Although some states require this diagnosis to be made by medical personnel (e.g., pediatrician, psychiatrist, neurologist), or psychologists, all diagnoses should involve an interdisciplinary team (Neisworth & Bagnato, 2000). The rationale is that interdisciplinary teams provide complementary perspectives that can strengthen the diagnostic decision and subsequent intervention planning.

*Interdisciplinary teams provide complementary perspectives that can strengthen the diagnostic decision and subsequent intervention planning.*

The "gold standard" instruments for diagnosis of ASD are the Autism Diagnostic Observation Schedule (ADOS; Lord, Rutter, DiLavore, & Risi, 1999) and the Autism Diagnostic Interview–Revised (Rutter, Le Couteur, & Lord, 2003). A toddler version of the ADOS is under development (Luyster et al., in press). The recently revised Childhood Autism Rating Scale (Schopler, Van Bourgondien, Wellman, & Love, 2009), in wide use over the last 30 years, is based on observation and generates a rating of autism and its severity. For early diagnosis, Bryson, Zwaigenbaum, McDermott, Rombough, and Brian (2008) developed the Autism Observation Scale for Infants, which can be administered in 20 minutes.

Diagnosis is a necessary first step in intervention planning due to its importance in establishing eligibility for services and funding. Diagnostic evaluations provide only very general guidance for intervention and further information is needed from the family (i.e., their priorities for the child), educational assessments, or requirements of the child's future education settings. Information on characteristics of ASD may also provide general guidance to service providers about particular areas of need, and some assessments are designed to generate educationally relevant information. These include the Autism Screening Instrument for Educational Planning (Krug, Arick, & Almond, 1993), the Psycheducational Profile (Schopler, Lansing, Reichler, & Marcus, 2005), and the Assessment of Basic Language and Learning Skills (Partington, 2006). Some comprehensive service models have established extensive curricula for children with ASD (e.g., the SCERTS model [Prizant et al., 2006]) and these can provide further guidance for planning. Finally, recommended practices in assessing young children with disabilities (Neisworth & Bagnato, 2000) apply to young children for ASD.

## Conclusion

Great strides have been made in the early identification of children with ASD. Public awareness and early screening efforts are finding suspected ASD in children at earlier ages, and diagnostic instruments and processes appropriate for young children are confirming these conditions. These important first steps are supplemented by educational assessment for informed intervention planning. From such plans, early intervention and early childhood special education service providers should build individualized programs for children and families that include practices with evidence of efficacy from the scientific literature. The subsequent chapters in this monograph will provide much information about those evidence-based practices.

## Note

Samuel Odom can be reached by e-mail at slodom@unc.edu.

## References

American Psychiatric Association (APA). (2000). *Diagnostic and statistical manual of mental disorders* (4th ed., text rev.). Washington DC: Author.

Asperger, H. (1991). "Autistic psychopathology" in childhood. In U. Firth (Ed.), *Autism and Asperger syndrome* (pp. 37-92). New York: Cambridge University Press. Translated and annotated from H. Asperger. (1944). Die "Autistischen Psychopathen" im Kindesalter. *Archiv fur Psychiatrie und Nervenkrankheiten, 177*, 76-136.

Baron-Cohen, S., Allen, J., & Gillberg, C. (1992). Can autism be detected at 18 months? The needle, the haystack, and the CHAT. *British Journal of Psychiatry, 161*, 839-843.

Bettelheim, B. (1967). *The empty fortress: Infantile autism and the birth of the self.* New York: The Free Press.

Boyd, B. A., Odom, S. L., Humphreys, E. P., & Sam, A. M. (2010). Infants and toddlers with autism spectrum disorders: Identification and early intervention. *Journal of Early Intervention, 32*, 75-98.

California Department of Developmental Services. (2002). *Autism spectrum disorders: Best practice guidelines for screening, diagnosis, and assessment.* Sacramento, CA: Author. Retrieved August 1, 2010, from http://www.ddhealthinfo.org

Centers for Disease Control and Prevention (CDC). (2009). Prevalence of autism spectrum disorders— autism and developmental disabilities. *MMWR Surveillance Summaries, 58*(SS-10), 1-20. Retrieved August 1, 2010, from http://www.cdc.gov/mmwr/indss_2009.html

Centers for Disease Control and Prevention (CDC). (2010). *Learn the signs. Act early.* Retrieved August 1, 2010, from http://www.cdc.gov/ncbddd/actearly/concerned.html

Dawson, G. (2008). Early behavioral intervention, brain plasticity, and the prevention of autism spectrum disorder. *Development and Psychopathology, 20*, 775-803.

Editors of *Lancet*. (2010). Retraction—ileal-lymphoid-nodular hyperplasia, nonspecific colitis, and pervasive developmental disorder in children. *Lancet, 375*, 445.

Filipek, P. A., Accardo, P. J., Ashwal, S., Baranek, G. T., Cook, E. H., Dawson, G., et al. (2000). Practice parameters: Screening and diagnosis of autism. *Neurology, 55*, 468-479.

Fombonne, E. (2009). Epidemiology of pervasive developmental disorders. *Pediatric Research, 65*, 591-598.

Interactive Autism Network. (2010). From first concern to diagnosis and beyond. *International Autism Network Report #13.* Retrieved August 2, 2010, from http://www.iancommunity.org/cs/ian_research_reports/ian_research_report_13

Hyman, S. L. & Towbin, K. E. (2007). Autism spectrum disorders. In M. Batshaw, L. Pellegrino, & N. Roizen (Eds.), *Children with disabilities* (6th ed., pp. 325-343). Baltimore: Brookes.

Kanner, L. (1943). Autistic disturbances of affective contact. *Nervous Child, 2*, 217-253.

Krug, D. A., Arick, J. R., & Almond, P. J. (1993). *Autism screening instrument for educational planning* (2nd ed.). Austin, TX: PRO-ED.

Landa, R. & Garrett-Mayer, E. (2006). Development in infants with autism spectrum disorders: A prospective study. *Journal of Child Psychology and Psychiatry, 47*, 629-638.

Lord, C., Risi, S., DiLavore, P. S., Shulman, C., Thurm, A., & Pickles, A. (2006). Autism from 2 to 9 years of age. *Archives of General Psychiatry, 63*, 694.

Lord, C., Rutter, M., DiLavore, P. C., & Risi, S. (2002). *Autism Diagnostic Observation Schedule.* Los Angeles: Western Psychological Services.

Lovaas, I. (1971). Considerations in the development of a behavioral treatment program for psychotic children. In D. Churchill, G. Alpern, & M. DeMyer (Eds.), *Infantile autism: Proceedings of the Indiana University Colloquium* (pp. 124-144). Springfield, IL: Charles C. Thomas.

Lovaas Institute. (2010). *The Lovaas approach.* Culver City, CA: Author. Retrieved August 1, 2010, from http://lovaas.com

Luyster, R., Gotham, K., Guthrie, W., Coffing, M., Petrak, R., Pierce, K., et al. (in press). The Autism Diagnostic Observation Schedule—Toddler module: A new module of a standardized diagnostic measure for autism spectrum disorders. *Journal of Autism and Developmental Disorders.*

Mandell, D. S., Novak, M. M., & Zubritsky, C. D. (2005). Factors associated with age of diagnosis among children with autism spectrum disorders. *Pediatrics, 116,* 1480-1486.

Mandell, D., Wiggins, L., Carpenter, L., Daniels, J., DiGuiseppi, C., Durkin, M., et al. (2009). Racial/ethnic disparities in the identification of children with autism spectrum disorders. *American Journal of Public Health, 99,* 493-498.

National Autism Center. (2009). *National standards report.* Randolph, MA: Author.

Neisworth, J. T. & Bagnato, S. J. (2000). Recommended practices in assessment. In S. Sandall, M. McLean, & B. Smith (Eds.), *DEC recommended practices in early intervention/early childhood special education* (pp. 17-27). Longmont, CO: Sopris West.

Partington, J. W. (2006). *The assessment of basic language and learning skills (ABLLS-R).* Pleasant Hill, CA: Behavior Analysis, Inc.

Odom, S. L., Boyd, B., Hall, L., & Hume, K. (2010). Evaluation of comprehensive treatment models for individuals with autism spectrum disorders. *Journal of Autism and Developmental Disorders, 40,* 425-436.

Odom, S. L., Colett-Kingenberg, L., Rogers, S., & Hatton, D. (2010). Evidence-based practices for children and youth with autism spectrum disorders. *Preventing School Failure, 54,* 275-282.

Odom, S. L., Rogers, S., McDougle, C. J., Hume, K., & McGee, G. (2007). Early intervention for children with autism spectrum disorder. In S. Odom, R. Horner, M. Snell, & J. Blacher (Eds.), *Handbook of developmental disabilities* (pp. 199-223). New York: Guilford Press.

Parker, S. K., Schwartz, B., Todd, J., & Pickering, L. K. (2004). Thimerosal-containing vaccines and autism spectrum disorder: A critical review of published original data. *Pediatrics, 114,* 793-804.

Reznick, J. S., Baranek, G. T., Reavis, S., Watson, L. R., & Crais, E. R. (2007). A parent-report instrument for identifying one-year-olds at risk for an eventual diagnosis of autism: The First Year Inventory. *Journal of Autism and Developmental Disorders, 37,* 1691-1710.

Robins, D. L., Fein, D., Barton, M. L., & Green, J. A. (2001). The Modified Checklist for Autism in Toddlers: An initial study investigating the early detection of autism and pervasive developmental disorders. *Journal of Autism and Developmental Disorders, 31,* 131-144.

Rutter, M., Le Couteur, A., & Lord, C. (2002). *Autism Diagnostic Interview—Revised.* Los Angeles: Western Psychological Services.

Schopler, E., Brehm, S. S., Kinsbourne, M., & Reichler, R. J. (1971). Effect of treatment structure on development in autistic children. *Archives of General Psychiatry, 24,* 415-421.

Schopler, E., Lansing, M. D., Reichler, R., & Marcus, L. M. (2005). *Psychoeducational profile* (3rd ed.). Austin, TX: PRO-ED.

Schopler, E., Van Bourgondien, M. E., Wellman, G. J., & Love, S. (2009). *Childhood Autism Rating Scale* (2nd ed.). Los Angeles: Western Psychological Services.

Stone, W. L., McMahon, C. R., & Henderson, L. M. (2008). Use of the Screening Tool for Autism in Two-Year-Olds (STAT) for children under 24 months. *Autism: The International Journal of Research and Practice, 12,* 557-573.

Swedo, S. (2010). *Report of the DSM-V Neurodevelopmental Disorders Work Group.* Washington, DC: American Psychiatric Association. Retrieved August 1, 2010, from http://www.psych.org/MainMenu/Research/DSMIV/DSMV/DSMRevisionActivities/DSM-V-Work-Group-Reports/Neurodevelopmental-Disorders-Work-Group-Report.aspx

Wakefield, A. J., Murch, S. H., Anthony, A., Linnell, J., Casson, D. M., Malik, M., et al. (1998). Ileal-lympoid-nodular hyperplasia, nonspecific colitis, and pervasive developmental disorder in children. *Lancet, 351,* 637-641.

Wetherby, A. M., Brosnan-Maddox, S., Peace, V., & Newton, L. (2008). Validation of the Infant-Toddler Checklist as a broadband screener for autism spectrum disorders from 9 to 24 months of age. *Autism: The International Journal of Research and Practice, 12,* 487-511.

Zahner, G., & Pauls, D. (1987). Epidemiological survey of infantile autism. In D. J. Cohen & A. M. Donnellan (Eds.), *Handbook of autism and pervasive developmental disorders* (pp. 199-207). Toronto: Wiley.

Zwaigenbaum, L., Bryson, S., Lord, C., Rogers, S., Carter, A., Carver L., et al. (2009). Clinical assessment and management of toddlers with suspected autism spectrum disorder: Insights from studies of high-risk infants. *Pediatrics, 123,* 1383-1391.

# Principles of Intervention for Young Children

## Implications for Toddlers and Preschoolers With Autism Spectrum Disorders

**Hannah H. Schertz, Ph.D.,**
Indiana University, Bloomington

**J**ennifer *is an experienced early intervention provider who recently learned from Christa, Jacob's mother, of his autism diagnosis. He is 26 months old. Jennifer was familiar with early signs of autism spectrum disorders (ASD) and this had led her to suggest an evaluation. For other toddlers with ASD, Jennifer has focused heavily on promoting social communication through relationships with their caregivers, using natural everyday activities. She feels most successful when parents come to appreciate their own ability to promote their children's development through parent-child interaction. Jennifer is aware that some recommend 40 hours weekly of structured individual intervention. She is confident that her approach produces good results for both children* and *their families, but this makes her wonder: Is autism a special case?*

Jennifer's unease concerns how to navigate the space that sometimes exists between evidence-based practices, intervention methods found to be effective through controlled research, and the broader recommended practices that guide her work. Early childhood professionals may ask: How do evidence-based practices stand up against standards that guide my practice? If very different approaches are effective, how can we best choose among them? Are effective practices for older children transportable to toddlers and their families? How can experimental methods from laboratory settings be adapted for the field? When research comes from fields outside early intervention (EI) or early childhood special education (ECSE), such questions about translating research practices for the field may be more pronounced.

This chapter provides a framework for exploring how to integrate *effective* practices with those that are *appropriate* for young children with ASD and their families. With respect to the latter, current recommendations of the Division for Early Childhood of the Council for Exceptional Children (DEC; Sandall, Hemmeter, Smith, & McLean, 2005) guide the field on issues of appropriateness related to intervention delivery. DEC drew from two sources to develop its recommendations: (1) intervention research and (2) the experience of stakeholders, including researchers, practitioners, and families. The first source of knowledge is concerned with "what works" and the second with the "how" of intervention. These recommendations are reviewed in the following sections.

## Five Principles of Intervention

The DEC recommended practices center around five areas of focus with importance for young children with ASD and their families. These areas are translated below into principles that relate to the family role, intervention environments, developmentally sound intervention, functional and child-initiated learning, and coordinated and systematic instruction.

### Principle 1: Intervention Is Family-Centered and Strengths-Based

*Jennifer shared research findings with Christa on how preverbal social engagement is associated with stronger language development and what it looks like (face-to-face engagement about something of mutual interest to the child and partner). She asked for Christa's ideas on Jacob's preferred toys and activities. Together, they planned ways to encourage Jacob to interact by looking at Christa's face during play and typical everyday activities. Christa's priorities were enriched by her new understanding of how toddlers learn to communicate. She was ready to support Jacob's learning in flexible ways that fit with his interests and with the family's values, preferences, and priorities. This approach also matched Christa's desire for Jacob to enjoy typical toddler experiences within the natural life of the family.*

Family-centered intervention is a central feature of Part C (Individuals With Disabilities Education Improvement Act [IDEIA], 2004), the law that guides EI for infants and toddlers with disabilities. However, the need for collaboration with families continues after the third birthday because families continue to play a central role. Family-centered intervention has three essential characteristics: incorporating family priorities, supporting a strong parent-child interactive relationship, and building the family's capacity to promote the child's development.

**Incorporating Family Priorities.** With their intimate knowledge of the child, families are well positioned to identify goals and activities that are functional and meaningful for the child and family. Professionals are responsible to enhance families' knowledge in ways that empower them and inform their priorities. For example, families' priorities may be influenced by enhanced knowledge of typical developmental patterns in social communication and specific ways young children with ASD are challenged to interact. In addition to their input on the content or outcomes of intervention, families' priorities for *how* intervention is conducted are equally important. This involves decisions on the intervention setting, services, how intervention is configured and coordinated, activities, and educational or other supports for families.

**Supporting the Parent-Child Relationship.** For toddlers with ASD, interventionists support the caregiver-child relationship rather than their own interaction with the child. For preschoolers as well, the parent-child relationship continues to be of central importance and, because social communication develops within natural interactions, failure to support and work within this relationship could squander a powerful medium for early learning. Jennifer viewed Christa's relationship with Jacob as important in its own right as well as for its role in his social communication learning.

*In family-centered practice, parents are not trained to function as therapists; rather, they promote the child's development through natural everyday interactions.*

**Enabling the Family to Promote the Child's Development.** Although the parent-child relationship serves as a critical foundation for social communication development, it is neither necessary nor appropriate that it be a didactic relationship. In family-centered practice, parents are not trained to function as therapists; rather, they promote the child's development through natural everyday interactions. Intervention builds on caregivers' strengths, arming them with knowledge about important next steps in the child's development and qualities of parent-child interaction that can promote them. This enables caregivers to focus their interactions flexibly to challenge the child's learning. Integrating child learning within existing relationships also enhances generalization of learning across the whole of the child's experience.

Supporting an active but natural role for the family to promote child learning has benefits for caregivers as well as for children. After actively participating in a parent-mediated intervention for toddlers with ASD that was more relationship-based than didactic, one parent described the personal benefit she experienced. "When I walk into a room, Ryan looks at me, smiles, and says 'Hi, Mommy.' I am a *person* now; better yet, I am a mommy again" (Schertz & Robb, 2006, p. 26).

## Principle 2: Intervention Is Implemented Through Natural and Inclusive Environments

In recommended practice, intervention is provided in natural environments. For infants and toddlers, Part C requires that intervention occur in home or community settings "that are natural or normal for the child's age peers who have no disabilities" (IDEIA, 2004, 34 C.F.R. §303.18) with justification required for any exceptions. In a joint position statement, DEC and NAEYC (2009) advocated for inclusive settings in which children with and without disabilities are represented in approximately the same proportion as in the general population.

**Natural Environments, Broadly Defined.** The U.S. Office of Special Education described the natural environment as the larger context of intervention that recognizes the capacity of families, supports caregivers rather than directly instructing children, provides coordinated team-based support, and reflects family preferences and beliefs (Workgroup on Principles and Practices in Natural Environments, 2007). Likewise, DEC promotes a broad understanding of inclusive and natural environments, defined as integrating intervention within socially grounded, natural relationships (e.g., parent-child, child-peer).

> *DEC promotes a broad understanding of inclusive and natural environments, defined as integrating intervenion within socially grounded, natural relationships (e.g., parent-child, child-peer).*

**Inclusive Settings.** According to recommended practice, inclusive settings are the first consideration for preschoolers with ASD rather than an option only for children considered "ready" for those environments. Inclusive environments provide natural opportunities for social engagement and friendships with peers, naturalistic social learning opportunities, language-rich venues with competent peer models for communication, and enriched opportunities for cognitive development. All are areas of critical importance for preschoolers with ASD.

Meaningful social communication, a central goal for young children with ASD, is more than a collection of individual skills learned in isolation; rather, learning occurs in the context of ongoing interactions that are not predictable or controlled. In inclusive settings, preschoolers with ASD spend time with peers who are skilled in social communication, giving them many opportunities to engage socially with a purpose and providing natural opportunities to support development of friendships. The social competence of their peers can serve as a natural scaffold or support as children with ASD learn to interact in a social world.

When compared with self-contained preschool classrooms, inclusive settings also "up the ante" for cognitive development because children with ASD are exposed to expectations aimed at a wider spectrum of abilities. Because children with ASD may be equally or more competent than typically developing peers in some learning domains, it is important that they have full access to opportunities that can support their individual interests and strengths as they also receive support with social communication, an area of greater challenge for them.

When intervention is provided in clinical or self-contained special education settings, these important social, communication, and cognitive benefits may be sacrificed. However, merely participating in inclusive settings is not sufficient for preschoolers with ASD because individual priorities for learning require a planful and individualized approach. Individualized learning can be promoted through a graduated system of support.

A first level of support follows universal design practices that may benefit all children as well as the child with ASD. These could include visual supports such as picture schedules available to all, calming areas to which children can retreat, or social supports that help any child to bridge challenges with peer interaction. Because they apply to all children, these practices are nonstigmatizing. In a second level of support, child-specific interventions not easily achievable through universal design can occur through individual accommodations such as visual scripts (Ganz & Flores, 2010) or interactive story telling (Whalon, Hanline, & Woods, 2007). Peer-mediated intervention is another individualized approach in which both children with ASD and identified peers are supported to interact in ways that target specific social communication outcomes for children with ASD (Odom, Rogers, McDougle, Hume, & McGee, 2007).

*Inclusive settings "up the ante" for cognitive development because children with ASD are exposed to expectations aimed at a wider spectrum of abilities.*

A third level provides separate activities specially designed for the child with ASD. For young children with complex needs, some advocate for a continuum of intervention in which intensively structured and individualized intervention may occur in separate settings. Others promote full inclusion for all children, albeit with more explicit, closely focused, and individually targeted intervention to address complex or intensive needs within inclusive settings. DEC and NAEYC recognize the need for a continuum of supports for young children with disabilities, but promote inclusion as a driving foundational principle (Division for Early Childhood & National Association for the Education of Young Children, 2009). Therefore, intervention should err on the side of inclusive practices that are integrated into the general activities of high-quality preschool classrooms and are accountable for achievement of important outcomes. If less than fully inclusive arrangements are pursued, they should result in superior outcomes without undue sacrifice to the child's and family's quality of life.

## Principle 3: Intervention Is Developmentally Sound

The third principle concerns the nature of the intervention with respect to the child's age and developmental status. Two aspects of developmentally sound intervention are appropriateness based on learning needs and preferences of young children (developmental appropriateness) and unique developmental variations experienced by toddlers and preschoolers with ASD.

**Developmental Appropriateness.** DEC recognizes that because learning is age-related, intervention is approached differently for toddlers and preschoolers than for older children. For young children, learning has a strong social component and is enhanced through play and engagement with peers and family. In addition to being more integrated within natural activities and interactions, the young child's learning is also integrated across learning domains (Copple & Bredekamp, 2009)—for example, addressing communication and cognitive goals within a social learning context. For young children with ASD, learning may be less effective if intervention addresses specific skills (e.g., vocabulary development or behavior compliance) in isolation of the natural environment and without relating learning to other developmental domains.

**Developmental Variations for Young Children With ASD.** Early intervention should take into account how social communication occurs in typical toddler development, how this pattern diverges in ASD, and at what ages these differences become noticeable. In the opening vignette, this knowledge helped Jennifer to recognize early signs of ASD, opening the door for appropriate intervention.

Typical patterns of early social communication development provide a guide for how intervention might be approached for toddlers with ASD. Preverbal social communication usually begins in early infancy with attending to others' faces and, by the end of the first year, joint attention appears (Bakeman & Adamson, 1984). *Joint attention* is sharing visual attention by exchanging looks between a partner and an object of mutual interest while showing social interest (Schertz, 2005). Research shows that once children begin engaging in joint attention, they usually progress quickly to verbal language, showing that joint attention serves as a "pivotal" competency by propelling a child toward further self-initiated learning and helping the child learn in flexible and functional ways (Bruinsma, Koegel, & Koegel, 2004). Joint attention presents special challenges for toddlers with ASD (Adamson, McArthur, Markov, Dunbar, & Bakeman, 2001).

> *Joint attention is sharing visual attention by exchanging looks between a partner and an object of mutual interest while showing social interest. . . . [It] presents special challenges for toddlers with ASD, but . . . can lay the groundwork for more natural development of verbal language.*

Armed with knowledge of the importance of joint attention, interventionists can lay the groundwork for more natural development of verbal language (Kasari, Paparella, Freeman, & Jahromi, 2008). In the next section, Christa engages Jacob in joint attention interaction through natural everyday interactions.

## Principle 4: Goals Are Functional and Oriented Toward Active Child Engagement

In DEC recommendations, intervention focuses on functional goals that promote child-initiated learning and active engagement with others. Linking to Principles 1 and 2, this is supported through naturally occurring activities with familiar people in familiar contexts based on goals that have meaning in the child's everyday activities. Examples are requesting a preferred toy or looking when a parent points to show something of interest (rather than naming objects from flash cards or rote counting). Goals are individualized for the child's environment, family cultural values, and child strengths and interests to ensure they serve a useful purpose in the child's daily life. For young children with ASD, interaction-based goals are especially important because they address an area of greatest challenge.

Dunst and his colleagues (2001) described how a functional approach to learning can meaningfully engage young children in development-

enhancing, everyday learning opportunities. Their research found that child outcomes were most likely to be achieved when learning opportunities focused on child interests, engagement, competence, and mastery. Jennifer's work with Christa illustrates how promoting preverbal social engagement (joint attention) supported functional learning for Jacob.

*With Jennifer's guidance, Christa focused daily on helping Jacob to engage with her in social ways. She began by helping him to feel more at ease when looking at her face. As he began looking at her more often (instead of only at toy cars—his preferred objects), Christa encouraged Jacob to share attention with her about his cars. She did this by looking pointedly at a car and then at him or by pointing to show a car to him. Soon, Jacob began to "show" cars to Christa by looking at them, then at her. She could tell that he was being social in these exchanges when he smiled at her. Christa found that Jacob seemed to feel success with this level of social interaction, whereas he had seemed frustrated earlier when she tried to get him to talk.*

Jacob's success seemed to follow from Christa's attention to his interests, engagement, competence, and mastery—the same components that Dunst and his colleagues (2001) found to be important to achieving EI outcomes. The use of familiar activities, interaction with a familiar person, and the choice of a developmentally accessible goal (joint attention) worked together to support Jacob's mastery of preverbal social communication in a way that was functionally meaningful.

## Principle 5: Intervention Is Coordinated and Systematic

The final principle concerns child-focused intervention. Recommendations address team-based and systematic practices.

**Coordinating Work in Teams.** Although the most significant area of challenge for young children with ASD is social communication, they usually have needs that affect other areas of development as well that may require the expertise of multiple professionals (National Research Council, 2001). Restrictive interests are a factor for all children with ASD, and challenging behaviors, environmental sensitivities, cognitive disabilities, and difficulties with feeding or sleeping may add further complications. In traditional practice, specialists provide parallel services in isolation from one another according to the child's areas of delay. An example is when a speech-language therapist provides pull-out speech-language services rather than working with the preschool teacher to support a child's communication goals in the social context of classroom interactions. This practice may encourage the teacher and family to defer to the specialist for communication intervention. It may also result in intervention that is duplicative, intrusive for children and families, and less than optimally effective.

In DEC recommended practice, intervention is provided through a transdisciplinary team process in which the team of professionals supports a primary interventionist and the family, allowing both to gain competency across all areas of intervention (McWilliam & Scott, 2001). Supporting professionals share their expertise more intensively in the beginning, gradually reduce their involvement as those closest to the child gain competence, and step back in with more intensive support in the case of setbacks or to address new goals. Through close monitoring, the team ensures that the quality of the intervention is maintained and that the child shows steady progress. A transdisciplinary team is more advanced than a multidisciplinary team in which team members work separately or an interdisciplinary team in which

*Supporting professionals share their expertise more intensively in the beginning, gradually reduce their involvement as those closest to the child gain competence, and step back in with more intensive support in the case of setbacks or to address new goals.*

members simply share information with one another while continuing to work in parallel fashion.

The National Research Council (2001) called for at least 25 hours per week of intervention for children with ASD. However, rather than defining intensity as a specific number of hours of professional contact, a transdisciplinary approach integrates intervention into natural activities. By providing support behind the scene, team members guide those who are constants in the child's life and who can promote child learning flexibly and nonintrusively across time and settings. Constant monitoring of child progress and stepping up involvement if needed are essential ingredients of high-quality transdisciplinary practice for young children with ASD.

**Systematic Intervention.** Intervention for young children with ASD may follow a developmental or behavioral perspective. When implemented with care, either provides a systematic guide for intervention and both have shown effectiveness for children with ASD (National Research Council, 2001); however, the two approaches follow somewhat different assumptions. Developmentally focused intervention is based on developmental research and emphasizes natural sequences of development as a guide for planning. Learning is viewed as transactional (i.e., socially embedded), influenced by the child's age, and integrated across learning domains (as opposed to promoting isolated skills). Following the child's interests and abilities, new learning is built systematically on existing child competencies rather than focusing on deficits in isolation (Copple & Bredekamp, 2009). Developmental principles of challenging children just beyond their current mastery level (i.e., the "zone of proximal development") and promoting socially based learning are supported by the theories of Vygotsky (1934/1986). Two developmentally oriented approaches to intervention for toddlers and preschoolers with ASD are the Early Start Denver Model (Rogers & Dawson, 2010) and the Early Social Interaction Project (Wetherby & Woods, 2006).

Behavioral intervention focuses on modifying (1) antecedents (what comes before a behavior) and (2) consequences or reinforcers (what follows a behavior) to systematically elicit or change targeted behaviors (Alberto & Troutman, 2008). Also, understanding the purpose that a problem behavior serves for a child can guide its replacement with a more appropriate behavior that serves a similar function for the child. Traditional behavioral interventions may use adult-directed strategies such as massed trials to influence targeted behaviors without regard for the child's natural environment or interests. Naturalistic behavioral strategies are more child-centered and take into account natural contexts for learning. Some behavioral interventions emphasize pivotal behaviors due

Table 1
**Principles of Practice and Suggested Indicators**

| Principles of practice | Suggested indicators |
|---|---|
| Intervention is family-centered and strengths-based | • Incorporates family priorities for intervention content and process<br>• Supports natural rather than didactic parent-child relationships<br>• Enhances families' knowledge to enhance their ability to promote the child's development |
| Intervention is implemented through natural and inclusive environments. | • Occurs in natural home- or community-based settings<br>• Places children with disabilities in group settings in similar proportion to the general population<br>• Is integrated within typical experiences and natural relationships<br>• Exposes children to rich experiences, building on strengths as well as addressing challenges<br>• Accommodates individual needs through a graduated system of support |
| Intervention is developmentally sound | • Is developmentally appropriate for young children, socially situated, and integrated across developmental domains<br>• Is developmentally accessible (near the child's current skill level)<br>• Addresses developmental foundations of social communication, promoting preverbal social engagement as a foundation for language |
| Goals are functional and oriented toward active child engagement | • Promotes child initiation and active participation in learning rather than relying solely on child responses<br>• Integrates learning into everyday activities with familiar people |
| Intervention is coordinated and systematic | • Is cross-disciplinary in focus, minimizing the need for pull-out or narrowly delineated services<br>• Promotes learning through behavioral and/or developmental proven practices; is planned and delivered systematically |

to their widespread effects on motivation for learning (Koegel, Koegel, & Brookman, 2005). Regardless of the forms that behavioral interventions take, specific strategies such as reinforcement, prompting, fading, and time-delay are used to support behavioral change. Project DATA for Toddlers (Boulware, Schwartz, Sandall, & McBride, 2006) and the Learning Experiences and Alternative Program (LEAP; Strain & Hoyson, 2000) are examples of behaviorally oriented approaches to intervention for young children with ASD that incorporate full or partial participation in natural settings.

Of course, although their underlying assumptions may differ, high-quality developmentally and behaviorally oriented interventions share common features. For example, just as developmental intervention targets the zone of proximal development, behavioral intervention considers children's current skills as they plan next steps (such as with pivotal learning goals). Similarly, developmentally oriented interventionists arrange the environment (i.e., antecedents) and use natural consequences to achieve learning goals. Systematic practices provide a framework for all stages of intervention from assessing, planning, implementing, and monitoring to revising intervention plans.

## Summary

In this chapter five principles guide EI and ECSE providers toward recommended practices in their work with toddlers and preschoolers with ASD and their families. Evidence that an intervention practice results in positive outcomes in a particular skill area is a necessary but not sufficient consideration for toddler and preschool interventions. These principles of practice do not replace evidence-based practices that have been shown by research to result in important outcomes for young children with ASD. Rather, they provide guidance for how evidence-based practices can be implemented within the fuller context of young children's and families' lives. The five principles can help interventionists choose among different evidence-based practices and adapt promising practices in ways that are most appropriate for toddlers and preschoolers with ASD and their families.

### Note

Hannah Schertz may be reached by e-mail at hschertz@indiana.edu.

### References

Adamson, L. B., McArthur, D., Markov, Y., Dunbar, B., & Bakeman, R. (2001). Autism and joint attention: Young children's responses to maternal bids. *Journal of Applied Developmental Psychology, 22,* 439-453.

Alberto, P. A. & Troutman, A. C. (2008). *Applied behavior analysis for teachers* (8th ed.). Upper Saddle River, NJ: Prentice Hall.

Bakeman, R. & Adamson, L. B. (1984). Coordinating attention to people and objects in mother-infant and peer-infant Interaction. *Child Development, 55,* 1278.

Boulware, G.-L., Schwartz, I. S., Sandall, S. R., & McBride, B. J. (2006). Project DATA for toddlers: An inclusive approach to very young children with autism spectrum disorder. *Topics in Early Childhood Special Education, 26,* 94-105.

Bruinsma, Y., Koegel, R. L., & Koegel, L. K. (2004). Joint attention and children with autism: A review of the literature. *Mental Retardation & Developmental Disabilities Research Reviews, 10*, 169-175.

Copple, C. & Bredekamp, S. (Eds.) (2009). *Developmentally appropriate practice in early childhood programs serving children from birth through age 8* (3rd ed.). Washington, DC: National Association for the Education of Young Children.

Division for Early Childhood & National Association for the Education of Young Children (2009). *Early childhood inclusion: A joint position statement.* Retrieved August 1, 2010 from http://dec-sped.org

Dunst, C. J., Bruder, M. B., Triveffe, C. M., Hamby, D., Raab, M., & McLean, M. (2001). Characteristics and consequences of everyday natural learning opportunities. *Topics in Early Childhood Special Education, 21*, 68.

Ganz, J. B. & Flores, M. M. (2010). Supporting the play of preschoolers with autism spectrum disorders: Implementation of visual scripts. *Young Exceptional Children, 13*(2), 58-70.

Individuals With Disabilities Education Improvement Act of 2004, 20 U.S.C. § 1400 *et seq.* (2004). Retrieved August 1, 2010 from http://www.copyright.gov/legislation/pl108-446.pdf

Kasari, C., Paparella, T., Freeman, S., & Jahromi, L. B. (2008). Language outcome in autism: Randomized comparison of joint attention and play interventions. *Journal of Consulting & Clinical Psychology, 76*, 125-137.

Koegel, L. K., Koegel, R. L., & Brookman, L. (2005). Child-initiated interactions that are pivotal in intervention for children with autism. In E. D. Hibbs & P. S. Jensen (Eds.), *Psychosocial treatments for child and adolescent disorders: Empirically based strategies for clinical practice* (2nd ed., pp. 633-657). Washington, DC: American Psychological Association.

McWilliam, R. A. & Scott, S. (2001). A support approach to early intervention: A three-part framework. *Infants and Young Children, 13*, 55-66.

National Research Council. (2001). *Educating children with autism.* Washington, DC: National Academy Press.

Odom, S. L., Rogers, S. J., McDougle, C. J., Hume, K., & McGee, G. (2007). Early intervention for children with autism spectrum disorder. In S. L. Odom, R. H. Horner, M. E. Snell, & J. Blacher (Eds.), *Handbook of developmental disabilities* (pp. 159-246) . New York: Guilford Press.

Rogers, S. J. (2010). *Early Start Denver Model for young children with autism: Promoting language, learning, and engagement.* New York: Guilford Press.

Sandall, S. R., Hemmeter, M. L., Smith, B. J., & McLean, M. E. (2005). *DEC recommended practices: A comprehensive guide for practical application in early intervention/early childhood special education.* Missoula, MT: Division for Early Childhood (DEC), Council for Exceptional Children.

Schertz, H. H. (2005). Joint attention. In J. T. Neisworth & P. S. Wolfe (Eds.), *The autism encyclopedia* (p. 115). Baltimore: Brookes.

Schertz, H. H. & Robb, M. (2006). Interventions for toddlers with autism: Building on the parent-child relationship to promote joint attention. *Young Exceptional Children, 9*(3), 20-27.

Strain, P. S. & Hoyson, M. (2000). The need for longitudinal intensive social skill intervention: LEAP follow-up outcomes for children with autism. *Topics in Early Childhood Special Education, 20*, 116.

Vygotsky, L. (1986). *Thought and language* (A. Kozulin, Trans.). Cambridge, MA: MIT Press. (Original work published 1934).

Wetherby, A. M. & Woods, J. J. (2006). Early social interaction project for children with autism spectrum disorders beginning in the second year of life: A preliminary study. *Topics in Early Childhood Special Education, 26*, 67-82.

Whalon, K., Hanline, M. F., & Woods, J. (2007). Using interactive storybook reading to increase language and literacy skills of children with autism spectrum disorder. *Young Exceptional Children, 11*(1), 16-26.

Workgroup on Principles and Practices in Natural Environments. (2007). Mission and principles for providing services in natural environments. *OSEP TA Community of Practice—Part C. Settings.* Retrieved August 1, 2010, from http://www.nectac.org/topics/families/families.asp

# Parent Voices: Early Experiences With Autism

In this chapter, three parents of young children with autism spectrum disorders (ASD) share their experiences. Chapter 2 of this monograph describes family-centered intervention as a guiding principle. The perspectives and insights offered here have important implications for the underpinnings of family-centered approaches: actively including families on the intervention team, addressing family priorities, and supporting families to promote their children's development naturally within the parent-child relationship. Although each author's story reflects unique cultural or familial values and experiences, common themes are highlighted in the boxes. The repeated appearance of these themes heightens their importance for the field.

*The Editors*

*Some names have been changed.

## A Mother of Four

I am the mother of three children with autism. I am also the mother of an infant who is showing the subtle early signs of autism. As I write this, I am surprised at how effortlessly I define myself as the parent of multiple children with autism. It has taken me many years to recalibrate my image of myself and my family.

### Max

My eldest, Max, now age 8, was diagnosed with autism at age 2. In retrospect, there were many early warning signs that I had missed, but I was unable (and in many ways unwilling) to recognize what was unfolding before me. The first person to openly share concerns about his development was my mother-in-law, who noticed that at 15 months Max did not talk, imitate, or gesture to communicate and would engage obsessively with toys. Soon after, my sister-in-law expressed concern that we were constantly entertaining Max to keep him engaged. I dismissed both of their concerns; I considered myself more knowledgeable than they on the subject of autism, because as a teenager I had worked in a camp for children with special needs. Children with autism didn't make eye contact, didn't like to be touched, and did not connect with people. Max, on the other hand, loved to cuddle. He stared right into my eyes when I sang to him. He wouldn't even avert his gaze for a moment.

I also believed that Max didn't imitate because he was engaged in interests far more advanced—such as studying air vents from all possible angles or flipping CDs on the ground and examining the trajectory and spin. Although I recognized that we were indeed continually entertaining him, I theorized that because we were both working parents, we naturally intensified the time we spent with him. Because we were giving more, Max needed more. That was what I was willing to understand about the situation.

I read books that supported and perpetuated my beliefs and dismissed books that made me question them. I even dismissed his pediatrician, who said, "He might have autism. You should find a place to get him socialized."

*Early Signs* *"Max didn't imitate because he was engaged in interests far more advanced— such as studying air vents from all possible angles or flipping CDs on the ground and examining the trajectory and spin."*

*"We were puzzled when Michael did not respond to his name."*

*"She was fighting sleep, would cry for no apparent reason, and would stare off into space as if she saw something that we could not see."*

I recall the painful moment when I finally allowed the possibility that Max had autism to enter my mind. I was reading a brutally honest check-list in a book by Bryna Siegal that described Max precisely. The reality petrified me. Although I still couldn't utter the word *autism* to anyone close to me, including my husband and my family, I could turn to other parents, strangers who would not judge or feel distress about my son, and ask them what to do. Each told me to have Max diagnosed immediately, obtain intense and high-quality therapy, and never give up. They made me realize that there was hope. Given that there was no objective medical diagnostic test for autism with which I had been forced to reconcile, it was up to me to accept the reality before we could move forward. I needed to know there was hope before I could accept the truth. I could not believe in something that was both terrible and hopeless. But give me some hope, and I'll listen. When Max was ultimately diagnosed at age 2 by an experienced and kind pediatric neurologist, I was ready to fight. I have been fighting ever since.

I often think back, wondering what someone could have said to penetrate the layers of cognitive dissonance. Perhaps I just needed time. But I do believe that I could have been steered in the right direction earlier with a different approach. In retrospect, I believe that my son's pediatrician could have handled things differently; she was in the best position to have helped me. Had she had more information, a phone number of another parent or of the local interagency coordinating council, offered specific examples of hopeful stories, or spent more time understanding that I could not accept pain without hope, perhaps I could have accepted it earlier. Instead, she felt that I was not ready. I wish she had helped me become ready.

Ultimately, I punished *myself* for my error in judgment. After all, it is a parent's responsibility to be ready for anything. I blamed myself for not facing reality sooner and wondered what could have been the outcome had we mobilized at an earlier age. I could not accept my ignorance as an excuse. Ignorance is not a justification in the law, nor is it one in parenting. The self-criticism was as consuming as my denial had been.

### The Wait for Answers

*"When we expressed concerns . . . , we were told he was healthy and developing fine."*

*"There was an 8-month wait for an evaluation."*

Unfortunately, in the years to come, I would have additional opportunities to make up for my mistakes. The same week that Max was diagnosed with autism by a pediatric neurologist, I found out that I was pregnant with twins who would ultimately, 15 months after birth, be diagnosed with autism as well.

## Marci and Anne

Marci and Anne were born just shy of 37 weeks' gestation, and their technical prematurity became the excuse for all of their delays, which were global. Their gross motor and fine motor delays were most obvious, though before age 1 we were beginning to have concerns about the lack of imitation, poor receptive language skills, and absence of gesturing as well as their general passivity.

At this point, I had linked the concept of autism with anything Max was doing or not doing, so the fact that they seemed different from him was reassuring. However, although they were not showing signs of perseverative or ritualistic behaviors, which were pervasive with Max, the twins were not meeting developmental milestones or acquiring skills. At 13 months I began the assessment process, and by 15 months they were diagnosed with autism by the same pediatric neurologist who diagnosed Max. He was kind, but it was excruciating.

In this instance I felt a new kind of pain. This time, I did not have the mountain of denial to climb. I was prepared. But the image of three children in applied behavioral analysis therapy, occupational therapy, physical therapy, speech therapy . . . was beyond comprehension. The vision I had of motherhood was displaced by a new image, the CEO of an Autistic Family. There is something *qualitatively different* about being a parent of multiple children with autism. Many other parents I had met had one or more neurotypical children before having a child with autism. They had been able to see themselves as a mother and then face a new challenge. But having never had a typical parenting experience, I had difficulty defining my role as parent, advocate, therapist . . . who was I? I felt I was alone in creating a new paradigm. I could not figure out how to love unconditionally yet be unyielding about progress. I pondered endlessly the genetic convergence in my offspring, about my father, who struggled with generalized anxiety, my father-in-law with manic tendencies, my brother who had difficulty with pretend play and following directions as a child, about my spacey brother-in-law, and of course about myself, how the anxiety and depression associated with my son's diagnosis must have affected my twins in utero and after birth. It was all too much to bear. When those feelings crept up on me I tried to squelch them, reminding myself that they were counterproductive impulses. The goal was to get the job done, and I had a big job to do.

Max had already had a few years of intervention before I began intervention with the twins. Max was, and continues to be, a "tough nut," and it took nearly 2 years before I found the right practitioners and the com-

### Getting the News

*"[I needed] more information, a phone number of another parent . . . specific examples of hopeful stories."*

*"My wife dismissed [the testing] conclusions as not measuring anything meaningful. She also thought Michael was having a bad day."*

*"At that moment, I believed that my life and my child's life would never be the same."*

bined approach that would make him successful. Once I could accept that this was going to be a lifelong struggle for Max, I could take great pride in his successes, which over the course of the past few years have been vast and in many ways incalculable, beyond all expectations. With Max I focus simply on the next step and when we reach that, I revel in it. Max has deeply touched so many people—his teachers, his tutors, his peers, and most of all, his family. He is a pure soul who inspires everyone who is open to inspiration. It is not hard to see what his purpose is on this earth. He has already inspired more people than I could hope to in a lifetime. It is my job to keep him happy, healthy, learning, growing, and by doing so, perpetuate his destiny of inspiration.

Marci and Anne have had intense intervention and services for nearly 5 years and are now attending a private general education kindergarten without any classroom support. Today, Anne is indistinguishable from her peers (aside from being many years above age level academically), and we will soon be conducting testing to finalize her "graduation" from services. Marci, equally as advanced in academic areas, continues to have some residual social quirks and generalized anxiety that we are addressing. Although it is hard to break the habit of seeing Marci and Anne through the prism of autism, I find that each day I can breathe a little deeper, knowing that sometime soon this

### Self-Critical Introspection

*"I blamed myself for not facing reality sooner and wondered what could have been the outcome had we mobilized at an earlier age."*

*"We tended to attribute his unresponsiveness to our own wrongdoings."*

will likely be behind them. I look forward to ceremoniously burning their files and will invite other parents over to help fan the flames, to show them that there is always hope.

As if our story wasn't dramatic enough, despite our careful methods of prevention, I became pregnant with Zachary, now 11 months old. When I found out I was pregnant (and once I could resume normal respiration), I wondered what God's plan was for us with this pregnancy. Was this going to be our gift, a chance to parent a typically developing child, who could learn incidentally without intervention? Or was this going to clinch my lot in life, to fight for the success of a brood of children with autism? As the eternal optimist, I was certain it would be the former. But after 6 months when I started to question his development and received confirmation for my concerns by various practitioners, I realized I was wrong. He is far more advanced than any of my other children were at this age, so I am hopeful, though the emotional wound has been reopened. Through intense intervention that we have begun this week, I am hoping to enhance his prospects.

Today, I am happy and fulfilled, yet afraid. I have accepted my lot in life and feel lucky that I have had the opportunity to be a part of Max's inspirational story and my daughters' successes—I know that all of them will continue to touch people in incredible ways. I feel empowered by my experience and by the amazing talents and generosity of the practitioners whom I have in our lives. My marriage, having taken many turns throughout this process, is stronger than ever. Although the workload is essentially mine, we are a united front. Nevertheless, I live with fear about the future, most notably about who will watch over Max and ensure his happiness and safety after I am gone. I also wonder if and how autism will "stalk" my daughters, either as a label from their past history (though I have concealed their diagnosis from everyone, including them) or how genetics will take its toll on their future families. I worry about the baby, and what the future will bring for him.

I have learned that we all have a great strength in us that we may not know is there. I could never have anticipated this lot in life and could never have predicted that I could manage it. I have learned to accept my fate and my challenges with grace, and open my mind and heart to the meaningful lessons and blessings that always seem to accompany the greatest challenges.

## A Father's Story

My wife and I noticed something peculiar with our son Michael during the first few months of his life. We read about how infants recognized their names within the first few months, and we were puzzled when Michael did not respond to his name. We tended to attribute his unresponsiveness to our own wrongdoings. For example, we would often call him "Buddy" or "Baby," instead of his name. My wife argued that he must be confused by the different names. Additionally, we often mixed languages because we are both fluent in English and Chinese, and Michael's Chinese-speaking grandparents were frequent visitors.

Our pediatrician provided additional peace of mind. When we expressed concerns about Michael's development, we were told he was healthy and developing fine. Because he was our first child and neither of us had much experience with infants, we relied on the pediatrician for guidance and trusted her opinions.

Around this time, I read about autism in a magazine and thought about the possibility of Michael having this condition. However, after thinking that he didn't fit some of the criteria, I confidently dismissed it.

When Michael was just over a year old, a coworker—a high school nurse—seemed concerned that he was not walking and urged us to have him evaluated. My wife and I were initially puzzled by the concern but agreed to an evaluation at our local elementary school. The results were astonishing. The evaluators concluded that Michael lagged his peers in every area of development and, without further explanation, referred us for early intervention services. My wife dismissed their conclusions as not measuring anything meaningful. She also thought Michael was having a bad day during the evaluations and that he would be just fine.

Although neither of us agreed with the assessment results, we accepted the offered services. Michael was just over 18 months old when speech, occupational, physical, and play therapists each began weekly hour-long visits. Our role was to observe and apply the demonstrated techniques throughout the day.

Many times these therapy sessions seemed like work for Michael. He was not motivated by activities such as puzzles or sorting objects, and we tried motivating him with edibles. Sometimes he cried or ran off to hide when the therapist arrived. My wife and I were also unenthusiastic about these in-home therapies. We still believed that nothing was wrong and that Michael would eventually catch up with his peers. We felt that the therapy sessions were unnecessary and often boring. We half-heartedly implemented what we learned from the sessions.

Michael made some progress after 9 months of in-home therapies. However, he still lagged behind his peers and the gap seemed to be widening. He still did not produce any words. We believed that many problems could be ameliorated if he could talk. We believed that having the right speech therapist was crucial and we replaced several of them; one, who suggested Michael might never talk, lasted only a day. His speech therapists had different views about means of communication. Michael's motor and imitative skills seemed to prevent success with sign. Michael had better success communicating with the Picture Exchange Communication System (PECS) than with sign; however, it did not help him to progress toward verbal language.

Our frustration with Michael's lack of progress mounted, and we debated whether or not to have him evaluated. My wife opposed this, fearing a label that would follow him for the rest of his life. Additionally, a therapist warned us of high costs and inconclusive findings. The program director noted that although the agency would help pay for the evaluation, a diagnosis would not change the level of services we would receive.

We were also told that there was an 8-month wait for an evaluation. Even so, we felt the need to officially confirm that Michael did not have autism and arranged for an evaluation when he was 2 ½ years old. A team of medical professionals diagnosed Michael with severe autism and possible mental retardation. We were shocked and immediately denied the conclusions with explanations such as discomfort with the testing environment, the tests' lack of sensitivity to his true abilities, and the fact that the evaluators spent only 3 hours with him. We left with a detailed account of the evaluation, an analysis of the results, a reading list, and a guide to local services.

Our therapists were divided about the diagnosis. Those who agreed with the results said that it would have been inappropriate or uncomfortable to communicate this with us prior to the diagnosis. Several family members echoed similar thoughts.

As we continued to receive early intervention services, we read books on autism, searched the Internet, and attended parent support meetings. This information was diverse and overwhelming. Eventually we settled on the applied behavioral analysis (ABA) method, a scientifically proven intervention method for children with autism. After beginning ABA, we began to see positive outcomes. Michael's motivation and skills drastically increased. After some initial hesitancy, we fully embraced the approach.

*A Mismatch: Professional Goals, Parent Priorities, and Child Interests*

*"We felt that the therapy sessions were unnecessary and often boring. We half-heartedly implemented what we learned from the sessions."*

*"There was little to no communication from the teaching staff other than 'she's getting better.'"*

As time went by, we began to slowly accept Michael's autism. We had hopes of full recovery after reading others' promising accounts. We tried other interventions such diet, medications, and sensory integration therapy, but none delivered the anticipated results. Michael was still nonverbal, was very socially isolated, and had high sensory needs.

When Michael turned 3, we began transitioning him out of in-home intervention and into the school system. A nearby school district provided an intense, ABA-type of preschool for children with autism, and it seemed to fit well with what we considered appropriate. However, to attend this school, we had to sell our house and move to an apartment located within the district.

After several months with this special preschool, we were unsatisfied. Michael still had not developed speech. We were concerned that frequent days off disrupted the intensity of intervention we sought. Meanwhile, I was learning about a form of ABA called Verbal Behavior (VB) that focused on communication. We enrolled him in a private VB program to supplement his regular preschool program.

The VB intervention plan seemed to show immediate positive results. Michael's sign language improved, his verbalization increased, and he seemed to enjoy learning. We took him to the VB program whenever his preschool was closed and after school hours. Because we were very satisfied with the rapid results, we asked the preschool staff to implement some of the VB techniques, but they resisted. Frequent programming disagreements followed and we considered pulling him out of the school system to attend the VB center full time. However, the cost of attending this private program was high and our insurance company did not provide coverage.

After some research, we found several states that required insurance companies to cover costs associated with treating autism. This resulted in a move out of state where we had identified a VB center that Michael could attend full time. This center offered a 40-hour-per-week intensive program year-round. We believed that this would benefit him, and the out-of-pocket costs would be affordable for us. He was 4 when he started attending the new VB center.

Michael's verbalizations rapidly increased and he approximated several words. He also continued to work with sign language. We were pleased by these early gains; however, after several months, he appeared to plateau and, in some respects, to regress. He tended to "scroll" through his signs and words until producing the correct ones. After working on this problem without success, the center decided to deemphasize sign language and verbalization in favor of PECS, which Michael used with more success.

About halfway through the first year at the VB center, we decided to explore other intervention options, including Relationship Development Intervention (RDI), a developmental approach to intervention that contrasted with his previous behavioral interventions. We were interested in

### The Importance of Hope

"I needed to know there was hope before I could accept the truth."

"We believed that having the right speech therapist was crucial and we replaced several of them; one, who suggested Michael might never talk, lasted only a day."

RDI for its focus on meaningful relationships and higher-order thinking. RDI is a parent-focused program that helps with joint attention (social sharing of attention). We have been using RDI for about a year while Michael continues attending the VB center. We apply principles of RDI as much as we can at home and have seen his social communication improve over the course of the year. However, it is hard to pinpoint which intervention is responsible for this growth.

I recently took a graduate-level course on autism and learned of the benefits of learning alongside typical peers. This helped drive our decision to transition Michael back to public school. With Michael now 5 ½ years old, we completed our individualized education program meeting and left disappointed with their proposed level of services. Recommendations were for a self-contained classroom for most of the day where he would work on individual goals. We argued for a more inclusive placement and social skills training with typical peers, but the school would not promise any of these services until they conducted their own evaluation.

Because we are unhappy with this plan, he is still attending the VB center while we wait for the school's evaluation.

Our experiences with autism have brought us much joy and frustration. We slowly came to accept the fact that autism will always be part of our lives. Each stage brings new challenges, and we anticipate that this will continue. For us, Michael's happiness is what matters the most. We have carried this philosophy throughout all the struggles in our continued quest to provide him with the optimal level of education.

## A Mother's Journey

### La Tanya R. Douthard-Jones

Several dates in my life were monumental. February 5, 2004, is a day I will never forget. It is probably the most important day in my life other than my own birthday. It is the day that I really learned to love, to nurture . . . it was the day that my daughter Amaya was born. She was a beautiful and happy baby. On a fluke, she held her own bottle just a few days after birth. She sat up on her own, cut her first tooth, and began crawling early. She began walking on Christmas Day at 10 months. Our world could not have been more perfect.

One of the dates that I consider not-so-good is the day my hopes and dreams for my beautiful baby girl child came crashing down on my head, or so I thought. This was the day we received the end results of months of testing and learned that Amaya had autism.

Many months prior, before her second birthday, we believed that Amaya was functioning well. She was talking, playing well, learning to use the potty, and very social. While her father and I worked, she was with her sitter, who had a fully functioning day care within her home. We received notes daily of what Amaya did, what she said, and what she enjoyed the most. Amaya was a singer. She enjoyed music—listening, singing, and playing with the toy instruments. She loved her friends at day care and especially loved visiting with one of her friends.

A few months after her second birthday, my husband and I started noticing "strange" behaviors. She was fighting sleep, would cry for no apparent reason, and would stare off into space as if she saw something that we could not see. We didn't worry too much and convinced ourselves that it was probably just the "terrible twos." One month later, her sitter began sending notes home indicating that Amaya would not play with the other children; she seemed tired, wouldn't talk much, and stared at her hands a lot. She requested to talk with us.

When I met with the sitter, I could tell that she was nervous and did not want to hurt our feelings. It was a touchy subject and she wanted to proceed very delicately. She said she believed something was wrong with Amaya, not physically, but developmentally. She said she started noticing changes right after Amaya's second birthday; her behavior, verbal capabilities, and appetite changed, and she was no longer social with the other children.

No parents want to hear that something is wrong with their child. I was heartbroken, upset, and brought to tears. I packed Amaya up and told my husband I did not want her to go back to her sitter anymore. I took 2 days off from work while searching for a new sitter. During my time off, I cried and prayed. My husband knew how upset I was, and we discussed our options. We talked about how we too knew that something different was going on with Amaya and that it would be best to see her doctor.

***Navigating the Service System***

*"It took nearly 2 years before I found the right practitioners and the combined approach that would make him successful."*

*"We had to sell our house and move . . . within the district."*

*"We tried . . . diet, medications, and sensory integration therapy but none delivered the anticipated results."*

*"The tuition [was] well over $50,000."*

During our visit with Amaya's doctor, we discussed the sitter's concerns as well as our own. She evaluated Amaya but then referred us to a specialist who dealt with behavioral issues and seizures. Because we indicated that Amaya would stare off into space, we needed to rule out her having epilepsy. The specialist evaluated her and had us complete a series of surveys. After reviewing our answers, she said she believed that Amaya might have autism but needed more information to give a formal diagnosis. Tears immediately streamed from my eyes because I knew a tad about autism.

My exposure to the word *autism* happened many years ago. *Rain Man* was probably my first introduction to autism. There were other movies: *Cries From the Heart* and *Miracle Run*. Although I had seen these movies, I did not relate the word *autism* to real-life situations. Due to my limited exposure to autism and not knowing some of the symptoms or early warning signs, I did not notice them with my own child.

Amaya underwent several types of neurological examinations and tests as well as eye, throat, and ear exams. She had blood tests, physical examinations, and other tests. When the results were finally in after several days, we were told that Amaya definitely had autism. At that moment, I believed that my life and my child's life would never be the same, that this would affect her socially, mentally, and verbally—possibly for the rest of her life—and that she may never grow to be an independent adult.

After a recommendation from the doctor to contact the state early intervention program, we scheduled a home visit. They too had us complete questionnaires and took copies of her medical records. After approximately a week, we were told that because Amaya would soon turn 3, we needed to contact our local school district, which was responsible to help children who have turned 3. I was frustrated when I realized I would have to rely on our steadily declining local school district to help my child.

We contacted the school district and were soon scheduled for another set of evaluations and questionnaires. Amaya was observed doing tasks such as jumping, running, stacking, grasping, counting, and speaking. While she was being observed, I met with the psychologist to discuss the results of the questionnaires and to discuss treatment options and school choices.

Amaya could not start school until she turned 3 and had her annual pediatric exam. She was finally placed in the first week of March 2007. I was terrified to leave my daughter in the hands of strangers, especially because she was barely communicating her needs to me. The prekindergarten program was a half-day program, so she would go to her sitter in the morning and to school in the afternoon. This did not prove to be a good situation. By the afternoon she was tired, wanting a nap, and not very open to the strangers at her new school.

I am not sure that the school was the best placement for Amaya. They allowed her to sleep and do other activities when she should have been participating in speech and group activities. There was little to no communication from the teaching staff other than "she's getting better."

Approximately a month into school, Amaya became ill and had to have hernia surgery, which removed her from school for more than a week. It was hard to get her back to being used to going to school. At that point, I knew there had to be a better school option.

I later learned of three local schools with great autism services. I began researching and contacting these schools for a visit. Little did I

**Empowerment**

*"I feel empowered by my experience . . . I have learned that we all have a great strength in us that we may not know is there."*

*"I now believe . . . I [can] help other families."*

know that I would end up visiting only one. There was a charge for Amaya to attend those schools, in comparison to the free option in the public schools. When I was told that the tuition for her to attend the first school would be well over $50,000, I was shocked and confused. I had to be clear with them that she was a 3-year-old and not a college student. When I found out that the tuition for the second school was also high, although not as high as the first one, I knew that my options for getting Amaya the help she really needed were dwindling. I finally contacted the third school and went for a visit. I instantly fell in love with the school and the staff. I knew this was the perfect placement for Amaya. The problem was the cost of $25,000—and it was only a half-day program. I began crying and asking God why this had to happen to me. The contact for the preschool program was very understanding and said she would help me figure out options.

I soon learned about the state autism scholarship program that would cover up to $20,000 of tuition. I was excited but still concerned about where the additional $5,000 would come from, in addition to day care costs.

However, it worked out and Amaya received a variety of interventions at the preschool. She loved it and regained her verbal capabilities, was potty trained, and became a little bit more independent.

As the old saying goes, all good things come to an end. Amaya graduated from her preschool program in July 2009. As much as we wanted her to stay at the school, we could no longer afford to send her there. We still qualified for the $20,000 autism scholarship but the tuition more than doubled for full-day kindergarten. We could not afford to pay $30,000 per year out-of-pocket to supplement the autism scholarship. This was devastating, probably more so to me than to my husband. I had come to rely on the wonderful staff there and knew that Amaya was in a loving, safe environment for children with needs such as hers.

After fighting a losing battle with the public schools in an effort to keep Amaya at the private school, I began the task of finding her a school with an "appropriate" autism unit. I visited several that were lacking in the technology, services, and staff that Amaya needed and had become used to. Her former teacher visited several schools as well and helped me find what we considered the best fit for her in the public school district.

### From a Focus on Limitations to the Child's Happiness and Potential

*"Once I could accept that this was going to be a lifelong struggle for Max, I could take great pride in his successes."*

*"For us, Michael's happiness is what matters the most."*

*"I don't know what the future holds, but she is progressing nicely and I will do whatever I have to to help her."*

Amaya is now 6 years old, attending a full-day kindergarten program at a local elementary school. Before she left the private school, we were fortunate to receive some grant funding to purchase Amaya an augmentative speaking device. This device has helped Amaya regain her language skills and communicate her needs to others.

This journey has been long and tiring with ups and a lot of downs. I remember asking God, "Did this have to happen to my child and my family?" I now believe this happened so that I could help other families who are going through the same thing. This is not a death sentence, and perhaps Amaya will live a prosperous life. I don't know what the future holds, but she is progressing nicely and I will do whatever I have to to help her. I love her . . . she's my baby!

# Applying Evidence-Based Practices to Support Communication With Children Who Have Autism Spectrum Disorders

Ann P. Kaiser, Ph.D.,

Jennifer P. Nietfeld, M.A.,

Megan Y. Roberts, M.A., S.L.P.-C.C.C.,
Vanderbilt University, Nashville, TN

**D**anny is a 2½ year-old boy with red hair and bright blue eyes. His sweet smile can light up a room and makes him a favorite of his child care teachers and his family. He is an active little boy with interests in trains, puzzles, and small cars. Danny can play with his favorite toys and watch videos for long periods of time, but he does not engage in play with his older brother or with his peers at child care. He communicates with adults to request objects and sometimes assistance, but does not communicate to share his interests or to express enjoyment in his activities. He uses a small number of single words (go, more, no-no) and two short phrases ("no way," "all aboard") that he has learned from watching his favorite videos. Danny was recently diagnosed with autism spectrum disorder. Although he has many skills that are appropriate for his age, his parents are concerned about his infrequent and limited communication. Danny's parents want their son to learn verbal communication skills for a wide variety of reasons: to facilitate learning new cognitive and language-related skills, to ensure sufficient success in reading, math, and other academic areas so that he can be in a typical classroom when he enters school, to play with and eventually make friends with peers.

Communicating with others in everyday social interactions is challenging for children with autism spectrum disorders (ASD). One of the earliest indicators of ASD is delayed emergence of social communication skills. Late-emerging use of vocalizations to communicate along with gestures such as pointing, showing, and giving; difficulty following the attentional focus of another; and the absence of shared affect are indicative impairments in social communication even before the emergence of spoken language.

Limited interest in social communication may be at the foundation of the difficulties that children with autism have acquiring forms (e.g., signs, words, sentences) and functions (e.g., greeting, commenting, sharing affect, seeking information) for communication. Children with ASD are less motivated to engage in the everyday social exchanges with adults and peers than typical children, and it is within these everyday interactions that language is learned and refined.

> *Children with ASD are less motivated to engage in the everyday social exchanges with adults and peers than typical children, and it is within these everyday interactions that language is learned and refined.*

Many children with ASD do learn to speak and to use relatively complex language, but a significant proportion of children do not communicate fluently enough in social interactions to be considered "talkers."

Fluency in communication comes from experiencing the success of more precise communication. For example, across many practice opportunities, Danny's sister Caitlyn has learned different ways to ask her parents for a snack ("I'm hungry." "Do you think it is time for lunch yet?" "I would like some animal crackers, please."). She now uses the forms of request that work best with her parents to specify her preferences so that she gets what she wants. Low rates of peer interaction make it especially difficult for children to fine-tune their social and verbal behavior so that it is effective. When children have low rates of engagement with peers, they have relatively fewer opportunities to observe, practice, and refine their peer-specific social skills.

More than two decades of research on naturalistic, early-communication intervention strategies have produced evidence that children with ASD can be taught new prelinguistic and linguistic communication skills (Hancock & Kaiser, in press). In this paper, we focus on variants of milieu teaching as a primary example of naturalistic communication interventions (e.g., prelinguistic milieu teaching [PMT], Yoder & Stone, 2006; enhanced milieu teaching [EMT], Kaiser & Hancock, 2002). Milieu teaching combines strategies for environmental arrangement, responsive interaction, and prompting communication in functional contexts. Environmental arrangement is a set of nonverbal strategies used to cue child social communication that include

materials of interest, toys out of reach, silly situations, sabotage, and activities requiring assistance (Ostrosky & Kaiser, 1991). Responsive interaction strategies include balancing communicative turns, responding meaningfully to children's verbal and nonverbal communication, and modeling and expanding language and play. Other evidence-based interventions share many of the tenets of naturalistic teaching (pivotal response training [PRT], Koegel, Koegel, & Carter, 1999; family guided routines-based interventions [FGRBI], Woods, Kashinath, & Goldstein, 2006). The principles of naturalistic teaching have been recognized as an effective component of early intervention for children with ASD (Rogers, 2006). Other early interventions that teach skills related to early communication (such as symbolic play and joint attention) but do not directly target verbal communication also have been shown to have positive effects on language (e.g., Kasari, Paparella, Freeman, & Jahromi, 2008).

Although the evidence that children with ASD can acquire new forms of communication as a result of naturalistic teaching is generally positive, promoting generalization across settings and partners and ensuring that children learn generative, flexible use of new communication forms are continuing concerns (Goldstein, 2002). Many children with ASD learn new communication forms and functions slowly during intervention and have difficulty using newly learned forms of social communication in flexible ways. Established patterns of social interaction such as low-frequency communication; absence of social signaling through eye contact, proximity, and body orientation; and inflexible patterns of language use such as echolalia and using "chunks" of language rather than generative combinations of words to convey meaning are not easily changed and may interfere with the use of new communication forms.

For children with ASD, there is evidence suggesting that earlier intervention is important to establishing functional communication skills (Lord & McGee, 2001), and intervention before age 3 is increasingly common. With early identification comes the need for interventions that are developmentally appropriate for young children.

*Teaching in natural environments and including caregivers as partners in early intervention are . . . especially important for children with ASD.*

Teaching in natural environments and including caregivers as partners in early intervention are essential intervention conditions for all young children with special needs, but they are especially important for children with ASD.

## Communication is a social behavior

For young children with ASD, acquisition of the social aspects of communication is the particular challenge. Teaching in social contexts and building on the principles of social exchange and interaction are at the center of naturalistic teaching principles. Naturalistic teaching has specified the following instructional strategies: teaching to child interests, contingent imitation of child behavior as a context for modeling linguistic forms, modeling language in functional contexts, expanding child language toward more advanced forms of communication, and teaching prelinguistic and nonverbal means of communication to establish a social communicative basis for learning verbal communication. The next step in applying these instructional strategies is to more fully understand the everyday social context and the more complete integration of naturalistic strategies into everyday settings.

## Supporting Communication Development in Young Children With ASD: Applying Key Principles of Naturalistic Communication Intervention

Table 1 provides an overview of key principles for supporting communication development in young children with ASD. These principles derive from a social transactional view of communication learning (Bruner & Watson, 1983) and from naturalistic approaches to early communication intervention. We highlight how specific language teaching strategies are consistent with developmental principles and the specific adaptations that are appropriate for young children with ASD in everyday social interactions.

## Social Relationships Are the Context for Communication

The desire to communicate is strongest and communication is easiest in the context of a relationship with a responsive partner. Partners create the immediate context for social communication with their presence, their attention to the other's focus of attention, and communication bids. Partners who are intentionally responsive to children's attempts to communicate motivate children with ASD to attempt and continue communication. The positive effects of training adults to be responsive partners in social communicative interactions

*The desire to communicate is strongest and communication is easiest in the context of a relationship with a responsive partner.*

are well established (Hancock & Kaiser, in press). Teaching parents, teachers, and peers to maintain social contact, to engage in play and routines, and to talk as they engage with young children with ASD increases the frequency of social communication by these children. The importance of social relationships goes beyond the provision of responsive partners to support communication. Relationships are ongoing, whereas responsive interactions may be momentary. Relationships imply history and experience with the unique communication abilities of partners. When we intervene to make social relationships easier or stronger, and when we provide opportunities for new relationships through inclusion and supported participation, we build the contexts for communication development.

Two examples of supporting social relationships for Danny illustrate the link between relationship and communication. Parent-child relationships are the primary context for early communication. Everyday interactions with children with ASD may be challenging due to children's difficulties with emotion and behavior regulation, limited skills for self-care, and strong preferences for familiar routines, foods, objects, and people. In Danny's family, his relationship with his parents is strained by his behavioral difficulties in daily routines. Because eating, sleeping, and transitions are stressful and time consuming, there is very little time for Danny's working parents to play with him and enjoy him. Reviewing family routines, examining parental expectations for these times, and planning functional supports that allow communication and completion of routines in a timely manner was the first step toward strengthening the positive interactions between Danny and his parents. As family members understood the events that were likely to trigger his challenging behavior and became more effective at reading his communication signals, the parents' enjoyment of their son increased. The early interventionist provided guidance for routines and helped the parents see their child's unique personality in his attempts to communicate. Teaching the parents key responsiveness strategies associated with naturalistic communication intervention had the benefit of improving their interactions with Danny and also providing appropriate models of communication. As Danny's parents felt more competent in everyday routines and more connected in their interactions with him, both they and Danny became more motivated to spend time engaged in shared activities. When the early interventionist provided information about expanding Danny's play by matching his actions and adding new actions, the amount of time Danny and his parents spent playing increased. Although each of these intervention points were well within the range of the early interventionist's skills in supporting parents and teaching children, the additive effects of these small interventions were to build a stronger, more positive parent-child relationship.

At child care, Danny plays with his preferred activities in parallel with his peers. Left on his own, Danny rarely engages with other children or with teachers except when he has specific needs. Danny's teachers anticipate his reluctance to interact with others and systematically include Danny as a key participant in classroom activities and routines. They use environmental arrangement, modeling, verbal feedback, and peer-directed prompting to make sure that Danny's interactions with his peers are positive and frequent. In most activities, Danny is paired with a peer who is more socially skilled and who can model appropriate actions and comments. Proximity is necessary but rarely sufficient to promote peer interactions among toddlers. Danny's teachers arrange the environment so that space, materials, and projects are shared. They encourage Danny to choose a friend, provide opportunities for him to give materials to others, and describe Danny's participation in positive terms for other children to hear. Prompts are given when there is a high probability that Danny will respond and when peers are in close proximity and likely to reciprocate. Danny has not yet developed friendships with his classmates, but he has many opportunities to engage with them in brief, positive interactions.

His teachers are laying an important foundation for his continuing social and communicative development by building early relationships with peers in his class. As his classmates' social and communicative skills develop, there will be opportunities to teach them strategies for interacting with Danny, but these are not yet developmentally appropriate for his toddler peers.

*Proximity is necessary but rarely sufficient to promote peer interactions among toddlers.*

## Nonverbal Interaction Provides a Foundation for Verbal Communication

In typical development, children communicate nonverbally and engage in nonverbal turn taking before they begin to use words and sentences. They also jointly attend, usually with a caregiver, to objects, activities, and events in their environments. During the early stages of verbal communication development, children continue to use nonverbal strategies, such as gestures, to clarify their communicative intent. For children with ASD, nonverbal as well as verbal communication patterns may be different. Joint attention emerges later and is less frequent in children with ASD. Gestures are used less frequently and in more restricted communicative contexts.

*Engagement in shared activities, joint play with objects, and nonverbal turn taking are forms of nonverbal interaction that provide an accessible foundation for building early communication.*

Nonverbal interaction, however, includes more than these intentional prelinguistic behaviors. Engagement in shared activities, joint play with objects, and nonverbal turn taking are forms of nonverbal interaction that provide an accessible foundation for building early communication. Naturalistic communication interventions promote nonverbal turn taking, situate adult-child interactions in preferred activities, and encourage adults to follow the child's lead and interest within activities.

When adults balance their verbal and nonverbal turn taking with children, respond to the children's nonverbal intentional communication activity, and provide models of gestures and joint attention, children's nonverbal and prelinguistic communication increases (Yoder & Stone, 2006). In addition, building symbolic play and joint attention can both increase these important nonverbal interactions and promote acquisition of spoken language (Kasari et al., 2008).

For Danny, increasing his opportunities for extended nonverbal interactions is especially important. At home, his parents and his early interventionist have examined daily routines and identified ways for Danny to participate nonverbally and to increase the number of nonverbal turns by Danny and his parents. For example, at bath time, a highly preferred activity for Danny, his dad offers choices of toys, suggests alternate sequences for washing body parts, and includes nonverbal play (e.g., racing boats, blowing bubbles). In the context of these engaging activities, vocal communication is frequent and there are opportunities for Danny's dad to model specific joint attention instances (pointing, showing, and giving) and words in context.

At school, Danny's teachers use similar strategies. They join Danny in play with trains and puzzles, taking turns nonverbally and modeling new play actions to extend their engagement. They use environmental arrangements to provide choices and to encourage Danny to communicate with gestures. At this point, they present choices or communication temptations (closed containers, materials in sight but out of reach) and respond to Danny's nonverbal behavior by giving him the requested object or action and labeling it. For example, a teacher may offer two toys at the water table, a boat and fish. When Danny reaches for the boat, she models "boat" and hands him the toy. She continues the interaction by joining Danny in racing boats and splashing. When possible, teachers include peers in making choices at the same time. Giving each child a turn to choose puts Danny's nonverbal choices in an easy social context. Teachers encourage nonverbal turn taking within activities. For example, at the water table, some children have containers to pour water and others have funnels and sieves for containing water. Danny likes both pouring and watching water pass through a big funnel, making it more likely that he will be a willing partner in these nonverbal interactions. In this context and others, teachers also prompt Danny to communicate nonverbally with peers (point to objects, show his work, give materials to others) and model nonverbal ways he can respond to his classmates (clapping for them, waving, and high-fiving with them).

At both home and child care, modeling joint attention is a good first step to accompany Danny's play and extended nonverbal interactions. Environmental arrangements that include novel interesting objects (e.g., windup toys in the water play), games where children take turns showing their cards with pictures of favorite objects, and opportunities to give other children materials at the beginning of an activity will support Danny in approximating initiated joint attention. Acknowledging Danny's uses of point, show, and give as communication will also encourage his use of these strategies.

## Children Learn Language by Communicating

Typically developing children learn language in the context of everyday interactions with caregivers and peers. Although children with ASD may require systematic instruction in communication, they also learn the form and use of language during their communicative interactions with others. For children like Danny who are low-rate communicators and reluctant partners in communicative interactions, the chances of learning from naturally occurring communication exchanges are limited. An initial goal for Danny is to increase the number of communicative exchanges he has with partners throughout the day at home and in child care. To do this may require environmental arrangements to increase Danny's interest in communicating and increasing his partners' responsiveness to Danny's nonverbal communication attempts and their skill at modeling language in response to his expressed intentions. By engaging Danny more frequently and for slightly longer periods of time (more communication turns), teachers greatly increase his opportunities to learn and use language. Helping Danny expand his play skills, embedding communication in daily routines, and arranging interactions with partners who can scaffold play into extended interactions also provide Danny with more opportunities to learn language by communicating.

## Children Fine-Tune Their Communication to Better Express Their Intentions in Everyday Interactions

The development of complex language depends on children's motivation to use more finely tuned forms in social interactions, as well as skills for understanding and learning the language system. For children with ASD, the motivation for fine-tuning language may be limited. Thus, it is important that the language modeled for them when they are socially engaged is tailored to help them expand and refine their language. Three aspects of naturalistic communication intervention help children with ASD learn more specific forms of language. Modeling related and/or more advanced language in response to their communication attempts teaches complex forms of language in the child's current context. A powerful sequence of teaching strategies are the provision of (1) slightly more advanced models, (2) contingent on the child's own communication, (3) in a functional context, and (4) followed by natural consequences for using the communication.

Fine-tuning communication for Danny, who currently uses only a few single words and rote phrases, involves providing specific labels for objects and actions. His parents routinely provide the names of toys, foods, and actions in response to his requests, and they expand Danny's use of "more" to include the name of the object requested ("more banana").

Increasing the number of different words Danny uses is the immediate goal because he has fewer than 10 different words. Both Danny's parents and teachers verbally label choices in response to his reaches to request objects ("Truck or train?"), follow through with a modeled word ("truck") corresponding with his choice, and wait for his attempt to imitate the model. They model the verbal label twice, always wait for his response, and provide the requested object to end the episode in a positive manner (See Kaiser & Grim [2003] for description of milieu teaching prompt episodes). Maintaining meaningful communication between Danny and his partner is the guiding principle in modeling within responsive conversations, expanding child utterances, and teaching only child-initiated requests. Because social communication is the primary challenge for children with ASD, meaningful communication always overrides teaching more complex forms.

**Using Naturalistic Teaching Strategies to Support Everyday Communication Promotes Communication Development.** Evidence-based naturalistic teaching strategies used to support social communication in everyday conversations can also promote communication development in children with ASD over time. The four principles laid out in this paper illustrate ways that parents and caregivers can use naturalistic teaching to help children with ASD become social communicators immediately and build communication competence one day at a time. As an ongoing approach to teaching communication skills to children with ASD, naturalistic teaching strategies in everyday environments offer unique benefits to the children and to their interventionists, making this mutually beneficial teaching and learning process a mirror image of normative caregiver-child transactions.

**Note**

Ann Kaiser can be reached by e-mail at ann.kaiser@vanderbilt.edu.

**References**

Bruner, J. S. & Watson, R. (1983). *Child's Talk*. New York: Norton.

Goldstein, H. (2002). Communication intervention for children with autism: A review of treatment efficacy. *Journal of Autism and Developmental Disorders, 32*, 373-396.

Hancock, T. B. & Kaiser, A. P. (2002). The effects of trainer-implemented enhanced milieu teaching on the social communication of children with autism. *Topics in Early Childhood Special Education, 22*, 39-54.

Hancock, T. B. & Kaiser, A. P. (in press). Implementing enhanced milieu teaching with children who have autism spectrum disorders. In P. Prelock & R. McCauley (Eds.), *Treatment of autism spectrum disorders: Evidence-based intervention strategies for communication and social interaction.* Baltimore: Brookes.

Kaiser, A. P. & Grim, J. C. (2005). Teaching functional communication skills. In M. Snell & F. Brown (Eds.), *Instruction of students with severe disabilities* (pp. 447-488). Upper Saddle River, NJ: Pearson.

Kasari, C., Paparella, T., Freeman, S., & Jahromi, L. B. (2008). Language outcome in autism: Randomized comparison of joint attention and play interventions. *Journal of Counseling and Clinical Psychology, 76*, 125-137.

Koegel, R. L., Koegel, L. K., & Carter, C. M. (1999). Pivotal teaching interactions for children with autism. *School Psychology Review, 28*, 576-594.

Lord, C. (2000). Commentary: Achievements and future direction for intervention research in communication and autism spectrum disorders. *Journal of Autism and Developmental Disorders, 30,* 393-398.

Lord, C. & McGee, J. (2001). *Educating Children With Autism.* Washington, DC: National Academy Press.

Ostrosky, M. M. & Kaiser, A. P. (1991). Preschool classroom environments that promote communication. *Teaching Exceptional Children, 23*(4), 6-10.

Rogers, S. J. (2006). Evidenced-based interventions for language development in young children with autism. In T. Charman & W. Stone (Eds.), *Social and communication development in autism spectrum disorders: Early identification, diagnosis and intervention* (pp. 143-179). New York: Guilford Press.

Woods, J., Kashinath, S., & Goldstein, H. (2004). Effects of embedding caregiver-implemented teaching strategies in daily routines on children's communication outcomes. *Journal of Early Intervention, 26,* 175-193.

Yoder, P. & Stone, W. L. (2006). Randomized comparison of two communication interventions for preschoolers with autism spectrum disorders. *Journal of Counseling and Clinical Psychology, 74,* 426-435.

Table 1

**Principles of Communication Development, Naturalistic Intervention, and Adaptations for Young Children With Autism Spectrum Disorders**

| Principles of communication development | Principles of naturalistic communication intervention | Evidence-based naturalistic strategies | Specific adaptations for young children with ASD |
|---|---|---|---|
| Social relationships are the context for communication | • Create a context for conversation<br><br>• Make responsive communication partners available | • Involve partners who already have social relationships with the child<br><br>• Teach partners to use specific responsive interaction strategies<br>• Respond when the child communicates<br>• Respond to the child's communicative intent<br>• Follow the child's topic and activity lead<br>• Talk about the child's focus of attention<br>• Mirror the child's actions and map joint actions with words | • Make social relationships easier in everyday contexts<br><br>• Strengthen parent-child relationships by addressing challenging behavior and daily routines<br>• Provide multiple opportunities for social relationships at the child's developmental level<br>• Support social relationships by teaching related skills to peers and others |

Table 1 (*continued*)

| Principles of communication development | Principles of naturalistic communication intervention | Evidence-based naturalistic strategies | Specific adaptations for young children with ASD |
|---|---|---|---|
| Nonverbal interactions provide a foundation for verbal communication | • Choose activities and materials of interest to promote nonverbal engagement | • Use environmental arrangement strategies<br>• Increase child engagement with materials, activities, and people | • Teach new object play skills to extend time engaged with materials and people<br>• Model and expand play actions |
| | • Promote nonverbal turn taking | • Balance child-adult nonverbal turns<br>• Mirror child's nonverbal actions and map with target language | • Create opportunities for nonverbal turn taking in routines and play<br>• Set up turn taking and exchanges within activities<br>• Use mirroring to sustain child-adult engagement or to gain child's attention to the activity and adult |
| | • Increase the child's use of joint attention strategies | • Model joint attention skills<br>• Respond to the child's nonverbal communication<br>• Make communicative attempts functional by responding with joint attention<br>• Keep communication going by responding verbally and nonverbally<br>• Balance positive responding with prompts for more complex forms | • Model specific joint attention skills: point, show, give<br>• Shape nonverbal communication toward joint attention |

Table 1 (continued)

| Principles of communication development | Principles of naturalistic communication intervention | Evidence-based naturalistic strategies | Specific adaptations for young children with ASD |
|---|---|---|---|
| Children learn language by communicating | • Increase opportunities for communication and learning | • Use environmental arrangement strategies to increase opportunities for communication<br>• Make partners available<br>• Choose materials and activities of interest to the child<br>• Increase opportunities for functional communication<br>• Increase opportunities for child-initiated communication<br>• Teach in everyday routines<br>• Use high levels of adult and peer responsiveness to increase child's frequency of communication | • Increase opportunities for both child, adult partners, and peers to communicate across settings and activities<br>• Ensure peers are proximal and there are functional opportunities for interaction<br>• Create opportunities for children with ASD and peers to manage materials for one another<br>• Use specific environmental arrangement strategies with time delays to promote child initiated communication<br>• Teach in routines that take advantage of proximity and share materials and activities<br>• Teach adults and peers strategies for being responsive to unique forms of communication of children with ASD |

Table 1 (*continued*)

| Principles of communication development | Principles of naturalistic communication intervention | Evidence-based naturalistic strategies | Specific adaptations for young children with ASD |
|---|---|---|---|
| Children fine-tune their communication to better express social intentions | • Model new forms in communicative contexts | • Model joint attention skills | • Continue to model prelinguistic nonverbal communication to promote higher rates of joint attention for children who are reluctant |
| | • Provide models slightly in advance of the child's current level of communication | • Model language at the child's specific target language level<br>• Model in response to children's specific communicative attempts<br>• Expand child utterances to add specificity and length<br>• Recast incomplete or incorrect words or phrases | • Model a range of forms for the same function<br>• Communication function takes precedence over modeling or prompting language |
| | • Use milieu teaching prompts in respond to child requests | • Use milieu teaching prompts using a least to most support sequence | • Balance prompting with modeling (1 prompt:4 models of the form). |

# Addressing Challenging Behaviors of Children With Autism Spectrum Disorders

**Glen Dunlap, Ph.D.,**
University of South Florida

**Phil Strain, Ph.D.,**

**Cheryl Ostryn, Ph.D.,**
University of Colorado, Denver

Children with a label of autism or autism spectrum disorders (ASDs) may be very different from one another. Some have intellectual disabilities, while others have typical intellectual development and some may even be gifted. Some speak in sentences, some use single words and gestures, some exhibit patterns of echolalia, and some do not speak at all. Some children with autism have challenging behaviors, and some do not. Of those children who have challenging behaviors, some have behaviors that are mild and easily managed, and others have behaviors that are more difficult, disruptive, and even violent.

Challenging behaviors are considered to be any pattern of behavior that interferes with optimal learning or positive social engagement with peers or adults (Smith & Fox, 2003). In this sense, they are defined on the basis of their effects. Common forms of challenging behaviors in young children with ASDs are tantrums, repetitive and stereotypic responding, disruptive noise making, withdrawal, and "tuning out" or lack of responsivity. Less common forms of challenging behaviors are aggression, property destruction, and self-injury.

Challenging behaviors are not a defining characteristic of ASDs, but it is true that many children with ASDs at one time or another will have behavior problems. Of course, challenging behaviors may be exhibited by any child, regardless of whether the child has ASD or not, but children with ASDs are at relatively greater risk for developing challenging behaviors due to their social, communicative, and/or perceptual disabilities. For this reason, it is recommended that teachers of children with ASDs be well prepared to understand, prevent, and intervene with challenging behaviors.

Although a great variety of approaches have been suggested for working with young children with ASDs, the dominant and most heavily researched strategies for addressing challenging behaviors emanate from a behavioral-educational perspective. The great majority of effective strategies for preventing and managing challenging behaviors are based on principles and procedures of social learning theory, behavior analysis, and positive behavior support (Conroy, Dunlap, Clarke, & Alter, 2005; Dunlap et al., 2006; Horner, Carr, Strain, Todd, & Reed, 2002). This is good news for teachers (and other caregivers) as behavioral-educational strategies are designed for application by typical professionals and nonprofessionals in classroom, home, and community settings.

## Important Points to Keep in Mind

Before considering strategies and approaches for addressing challenging behavior, it is useful to emphasize five basic foundational messages.

### Children With ASDs Are, First of All, Children

Children with challenging behaviors are, first and foremost, children. The point here is that the issue of challenging behaviors should never command so much focus that the needs, strengths, and interests of the child are neglected. Simply because a child may have challenging behaviors does not negate the importance of a comprehensive program geared to promote the child's healthy social, emotional, and intellectual development. In fact, the higher the quality of comprehensive guidance and instruction to promote healthy child development, the lower the probability that challenging behaviors will be a major concern.

*The issue of challenging behaviors should never command so much focus that the needs, strengths, and interests of the child are neglected.*

### Children Are Members of Families

The primary context for young children's development is the family and, so, efforts to address challenging behaviors (and, for that matter, any other behaviors) should be developed in partnership with the child's parents or other primary caregivers. Even when the primary concern is within the classroom, family members have much to contribute, especially in terms of their deep knowledge of the child's preferences, characteristics, strengths, and learning history.

## Children With ASDs, Like All Children, Are Social Beings

All important learning occurs in a social context, and essentially all meaningful activity in a child's future schooling and adult life will take place in social interactions. The most important goals of preschool education involve the development of social competencies and learning to develop friendships. Furthermore, challenging behaviors are social phenomena, and efforts to address them must involve social contexts and considerations.

*Challenging behaviors are social phenomena, and efforts to address them must involve social contexts and considerations.*

## Challenging Behaviors Occur for a Reason

The central point in understanding why challenging behaviors occur is to appreciate that they serve a purpose (or function) for the child. The purpose, generally stated, is to make something happen or not happen in the environment. The child may not be consciously aware of the purpose, and sometimes it may be difficult to figure it out; however, there is always an answer, and an understanding of the behavior's purpose can be of tremendous help in designing an effective resolution.

## The Best Ways to Address Challenging Behaviors Are Indirect

One of the most important conclusions from the past 3 decades of research on challenging behaviors is that the most effective methods of prevention and intervention involve practices that are implemented when the challenging behaviors are *not* occurring. These indirect methods include (1) the teaching of alternative communication and social skills so that the child does not need to resort to challenging behaviors and (2) arranging the environment to encourage desirable, prosocial responses and to prevent challenging behaviors (Dunlap & Carr, 2007).

*Challenging behaviors almost always can be interpreted as communication—their occurrence can mean that the child wants to get something or to get rid of something.*

Such indirect procedures have proven to be much more effective and longer lasting than direct interventions applied after a challenging behavior has occurred (e.g., time out, reprimands).

In the remainder of this article, we describe a framework for thinking about and organizing prevention and intervention strategies addressing challenging behavior for children with ASDs. A three-tiered model is presented and illustrated with a case study. The case study refers to some recommended practices; however, more detail and specific guidance is available in numerous articles, books (e.g., Luiselli, Russo, Christian, & Wilczynski, 2008), and Web sites (e.g., www.challengingbehavior.org; http://autismpdc.fpg.unc.edu).

## A Tiered Model for Thinking About Needed Services

The tiered model being advanced for children with ASDs is based on the three-level model of prevention that has been increasingly common in many arenas of social services, including public health and education (e.g., Fox, Dunlap, Hemmeter, Joseph, & Strain, 2003; Simeonsson, 1991; Sugai et al., 2000; Walker et al., 1996). The model begins by defining target behaviors in need of prevention, such as social isolation, destructive/disruptive behaviors by children with ASDs, or high levels of parental stress. Strategies intended to prevent the occurrence or further development of the target behaviors are then categorized along a hierarchy related to the proportion of the population for whom the strategy would be pertinent, the intensity of the strategy, and the stage of the target behavior's development.

Level 1 strategies are intended for the entire population of children and families affected by ASDs or challenging behaviors. The strategies are geared to an early stage of prevention and are relatively inexpensive and easy to implement. This level is referred to as primary prevention, involving universal applications. Level 1 begins with fundamental assurances for all children: safe and secure environments, positive and attentive parenting, and optimal physical health and nutrition. Other assurances are more specific to ASDs. For example, a universal strategy to prevent disruptive behavior might include a functional system of communication by which the child can readily express wants, needs, and irritants. A universal strategy to prevent parent stress that interferes with

*The most effective methods of prevention and intervention involve practices that are implemented when the challenging behaviors are not occurring.*

the child's development might include guided opportunities for family members to discuss issues they face with others in similar circumstances. Universal strategies for children with ASDs are implemented for all children and families, as early as possible.

Figure 1

**Tiered Intervention Model for Children With ASDs**

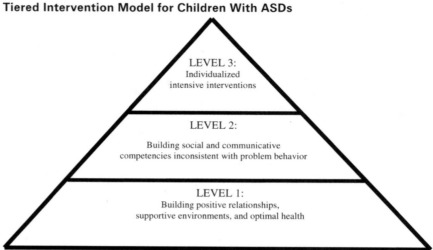

LEVEL 3:
Individualized
intensive interventions

LEVEL 2:

Building social and communicative
competencies inconsistent with problem behavior

LEVEL 1:
Building positive relationships,
supportive environments, and optimal health

Level 2 is referred to as secondary prevention. It is intended for individuals for whom Level 1 is insufficient and who are clearly at risk for, or who are already demonstrating, early signs of challenging behavior. For children with ASDs, Level 2 strategies might include teaching appropriate problem solving, self-regulation, and coping as a way to divert them from using problem behavior. As an example, a timer could be used to help a 2-year-old pause before accessing a requested item. This could be done during simple turn-taking routines with a family member such as requesting a favorite snack item and waiting 3 seconds for its delivery.

Level 2 strategies to prevent parental stress might include systematic, group training in strategies that make daily routines more enjoyable. Level 2 strategies are more focused than Level 1, involve a smaller proportion of the population, and are less intensive and costly than Level 3 strategies. Still, for children with ASDs, due to their substantial risk factors, it is likely that a relatively large segment of the population will require and benefit from Level 2 strategies.

Level 3 is for children who are already displaying serious behaviors and require relatively intensive and individualized interventions. This level, sometimes called tertiary prevention, involves individualized assessment and assessment-based interventions that are well represented in the literature on positive behavior support and applied behavior analysis. In Level 3, providers work with children and families on a one-to-one basis. These strategies are markedly more expensive in resources and time than Levels 1 or 2. It is important to clarify that Level 3 is not just one level of intensity. Procedures are implemented on a continuum of intensity based on the extent to which challenges are severe, long lasting, and resistant to change. For example, if a child is beginning to display tantrums at home, but the tantrums are limited to one or two daily occurrences and have not been exhibited in the community, the procedures need not be particularly time consuming or effortful (although they may still require individualized assessment and an individualized intervention plan). Similarly, if the child is only 2 years old with problem behaviors that have functions that are easily understood (i.e., seeking attention at mealtimes), they might call for a relatively straightforward and efficient process of intervention development and implementation (Dunlap & Fox, 1999; Strain & Schwartz, 2009). On the other hand, if a child has had severe problem behaviors for several months, and the problems have persisted in many environments despite multiple efforts of remediation, then the Level 3 process is likely to require a considerable investment of time and resources to be effective.

The multitiered prevention model is represented in Figure 1. The bottom tier, Level 1, is intended for all children with ASDs and other children with severe communication and/or behavioral delays, while Levels 2 and 3 build increasingly focused and intensive supports for those children who continue to exhibit challenging behavior even when the previous level of intervention/support has been provided. Across all three levels we suggest that strategies focus on six areas of concern: (1) health promotion, (2) functional communication, (3) safe and secure environment, (4) close family attachments, (5) learning environment that is engaging, and (6) parental stress reduction. The following case study presents an illustration of the application of the tiered model across these six areas of concern.

*Kevin is a 4½-year-old boy who recently received a diagnosis of ASD. His verbal language is more typical of a 3-year-old, and he regularly displays echolalia and a lack of concentration. Kevin shows aggression toward others by screaming, pushing, and kicking, especially when he does not want to comply with requests or his environment changes. A major concern is Kevin's daily self-injurious behaviors such as banging his fist to his temples or banging his right elbow on walls, chairs, and the floor. These behaviors have resulted in cuts, bruises, and swellings. Kevin has an older sister, Shannon, and a younger brother, Dillon. He lives in a small three bedroom town house and attends a community preschool program 3 days a week. Mom is the primary caregiver and dad works full time. Kevin's parents are concerned about his aggressive and self-injurious behaviors at preschool and home, especially as he shares a bedroom with 7-month-old Dillon.*

Table 1
**Family Behavioral Goals**

| Domain | Goals |
|---|---|
| Health | • Attend regular health visits<br>• Stop self-injurious behaviors<br>• (Schedule 6-month MRI if behavior continues) |
| Communication | • Use words instead of screams, pushes, and kicks<br>• Communicate wants and needs |
| Safe and secure home environment | • Calmly transition between activities<br>• Increase engagement in activities |
| Family attachments | • Engage in "family time"<br>• Play in the play area with his sister<br>• Demonstrate appropriate behaviors toward others<br>• Increase compliance in following instructions |
| Stimulating environments | • Demonstrate appropriate behaviors toward others<br>• Use language instead of inappropriate behaviors<br>• Follow teacher directions<br>• Stay quiet (no screaming) in community places and other people's houses |
| Parental stress | • Be involved in a support network<br>• Engage in respite<br>• Keep stress levels to a minimum<br>• Learn positive behavioral strategies to use with Kevin |

Table 2
**Level 1 Strategies for Meeting Behavioral Goals**

| Domain | Strategy |
|---|---|
| Health | Kevin attends regular well-child visits. His parents insisted on an MRI scan to rule out any brain damage from Kevin's self-injurious behaviors. The results were negative, but the neurologist strongly suggested addressing this behavior. |

Table 2 (*continued*)

| Domain | Strategy |
|---|---|
| Communication | Although Kevin is 24 months below his age in language development, he can communicate his message by using several two-word phrases strung together. |
| Safe and secure home environment | Kevin is currently sharing a bedroom with his infant brother, Dillon. Kevin's dad is planning to build an internal wall to make two rooms, but for now, there is a large screen in place allowing Kevin to have his own "space." Kevin has easy access to a large box of his favorite toys (vehicles) and he also has his own small TV and DVD player. There is a big breakfast bar in the kitchen where the family gathers for meals and a living room with a play area with toys and books. In the backyard there is a swing set and sand box. |
| Family attachments | Kevin is at home during the day with his mom and brother (when not at preschool), so there are times when Kevin is alone while mom attends to the baby. However, when Dillon is napping, Kevin's mom engages him in games, books, and activities for about 2 hours. Kevin's mom tries to use as much language as possible to help Kevin expand his vocabulary and tries to keep him calm during activity transitions. In the evenings, the whole family has dinner together and spends time in the living room until bedtime. Sometimes Kevin's dad will take him swimming or to play catch with a football. |
| Stimulating environments | Kevin attends a preschool three days a week, and sometimes his mom will take him to the park. On the weekends, the whole family will go hiking, fishing, sailing, or visiting family who live nearby. |
| Parental stress | Kevin's parents have respite care and choose to use one session to go out together; sometimes they take Dillon as he is still young. Both sides of the family live close, so they have a lot of support in the area. |

The Level 1 practices described previously resulted in significant behavioral improvement with Kevin. However, Level 2 practices were needed to further improve his communications, social, and engagement goals.

Table 3
**Level 2 Strategies for Meeting Behavioral Goals**

| Domain | Strategy |
|---|---|
| Health | Level 1 continuation |
| Communication | To eliminate Kevin's aggressive behavior toward others and self-injurious behaviors, he is taught appropriate, alternative phrases such as, "I don't want to go there," "I want to stay," and "five more minutes please." |
| Safe and secure home environment | Level 1 continuation |
| Family attachments | Kevin's mom and dad use verbal redirection or physical prompts (if necessary) to encourage Kevin to engage in activities. They also give him simple one-step directions (using physical prompts if necessary) and praise him for completion. These simple directions typically end with highly reinforcing consequences such as "Kevin, go get a cracker from the plate," after which he gets to eat the cracker (a natural consequence). |
| Stimulating environments | Kevin's teacher will also give Kevin simple one-step directions such as "Kevin, open the train box" (using physical prompts if necessary) and praising him for completion. Then he gets to play with his favorite train. Kevin is prompted to use newly learned phrases (see Communication) when he starts to scream, push, kick, or engage in self-injurious behaviors. Kevin's parents and teachers explicitly tell Kevin what activity is next such as "it's time for lunch now," to help him remain calm through transitions. |

Table 3 (*continued*)

| Domain | Strategy |
|---|---|
| Parental stress | Kevin's parents will increase their respite time and also ask family members to help out or babysit while they go out together or with friends. They will also arrange a day for a consultant to come and teach them new behavioral strategies to implement with Kevin. |

Not all strategies described previously in Level 2 were effective in eliminating Kevin's challenging behaviors, so his parents sought help from a consultant. The consultant who was trained in behavior analysis conducted a functional behavior assessment (FBA) of Kevin's challenging behaviors in order to determine their functions. The FBA was conducted by manipulating Kevin's environment (such as giving attention, and then not giving any attention) and recording the presence and absence of his challenging behaviors. The results of Kevin's FBA showed that his aggressive behavior a function of escape (wanting to get away from what was going on) and his self-injurious behavior served a function of wanting attention. The new behavioral strategies emanating from the FBA are highlighted on table 4. Please note the goals and strategies are interlinked among the domains.

Table 4
**Level 3 Strategies for Meeting Behavioral Goals**

| Domain | Strategy |
|---|---|
| Health | Level 1 continuation |
| Communication | To eliminate Kevin's aggressive behavior toward others and self-injurious behaviors, he is taught appropriate, alternative phrases such as, "I don't want to go there," "I want to stay," and "five more minutes please." In addition, Kevin's mom, dad, and teacher dedicate a few minutes at the start of the day to talk about the different activities in which Kevin will partake. He is also given a photographic schedule so he can visualize his day. They also talk to Kevin about the different things he can do during the activities, such as making a dinosaur during play-doh time at school or picking a train book from the library with Mom. Five minutes before each daily transition, Kevin is told about what is going to happen, so he can prepare himself for the next activity. |

Table 4 (*continued*)

| Domain | Strategy |
|---|---|
| Safe and secure home environment | Level 1 continuation |
| Family attachments | Kevin's mom or dad uses verbal redirection or physical prompts (if necessary) to encourage Kevin to engage in activities. Kevin's parents also give him simple one-step directions (using physical prompts if necessary) and praise him for completion. These simple directions can start in highly reinforcing consequences such as "Kevin, go get a cracker from the plate," and Kevin gets to eat the cracker (also a natural consequence). In addition, Kevin's family ensures they give him more attention and catch him "being good," such as praising him and giving him positive attention when he is sitting still, eating well, being quiet, and playing. By giving this extra attention before Kevin starts to display self-injurious behaviors (wanting attention), Kevin will not have to "act out" to get attention. |
| Stimulating environments | Kevin's teacher will also give Kevin simple one-step directions (using physical prompts if necessary) and praise him for completion, such as "Kevin, open the train box" and he gets to play with his favorite train. Kevin will be prompted to use one of the new phrases (see Communication) when he starts to scream, push, or kick. Also see photographic daily schedule in Communication. |
| Parental stress | Kevin's parents will increase their respite time, and also ask family members to help or babysit while they go out together or with friends. They will also arrange a day when the consultant can come over and teach them new behavioral strategies to implement with Kevin. Kevin's parents will inform family members and those people who interact with Kevin in the community about the new behavioral strategies so their implementation can remain consistent across settings, people, and times. Kevin's parents and teacher will learn how to collect behavioral data on his aggressive and self-injurious behaviors and with the help of the consultant, adapt Kevin's behavioral program over time as needed. |

# Summary

In this article we have argued for an ecologically valid, preventive, and multilevel approach to dealing with the challenging behaviors of young children with ASDs. We believe this approach is highly compatible with the Division for Early Childhood recommended practices, is responsive to the rapidly emerging use of Response to Intervention (RTI) in early childhood (see Fox et al., 2003), and holds the greatest promise for sustainable and generalized behavior change.

### Note

Glen Dunlap may be reached by e-mail at glendunlap@sbcglobal.net

Preparation of this manuscript was supported by the Technical Assistance Center for Social Emotional Interventions for Young Children, Office of Special Education Programs, U.S. Department of Education (H326B070002).

### References

Conroy, M. A., Dunlap, G., Clarke, S., & Alter, P. J. (2005). A descriptive analysis of positive behavioral intervention research with young children with challenging behavior. *Topics in Early Childhood Special Education, 25,* 157-166.

Dunlap, G. & Carr, E. G. (2007). Positive behavior support and developmental disabilities: A summary and analysis of research. In S. L. Odom, R. H. Horner, M. Snell, & J. Blacher (Eds.), *Handbook of developmental disabilities* (pp. 469-482). New York: Guilford.

Dunlap, G. & Fox, L. (1999). A demonstration of behavioral support for young children with autism. *Journal of Positive Behavior Interventions, 1,* 77-87.

Dunlap, G., Strain, P. S., Fox, L., Carta, J. J., Conroy, M., Smith, B., et al. (2006). Prevention and intervention with young children's challenging behavior: A summary and perspective regarding current knowledge. *Behavioral Disorders, 32,* 29-45.

Fox, L., Dunlap, G., Hemmeter, M. L., Joseph, G. E., & Strain, P. S. (2003). The teaching pyramid: A model for supporting social competence and preventing challenging behavior in young children. *Young Children, 58,* 48-52.

Horner, R. H., Carr, E. G., Strain, P. S., Todd, A. W., & Reed, H. K. (2002). Problem behavior interventions for young children with autism. *Journal of Autism and Developmental Disorders, 32,* 423-446.

Luiselli, J. K., Russo, D. C., Christian, W. P., & Wilczynski, S. M. (2008). *Effective practices for children with autism.* New York: Oxford University Press.

Simeonson, R. J. (1991). Primary, secondary, and tertiary prevention in early intervention. *Journal of Early Intervention, 15,* 124-134.

Smith, B. & Fox, L. (2003). *Systems of service delivery: A synthesis of evidence relevant to young children at risk of or who have challenging behavior.* Tampa: University of South Florida, Center for Evidence-Based Practice: Young Children with Challenging Behavior.

Strain, P. & Schwartz, I. (2009). Positive behavior support and early intervention for young children with autism: Case studies on the efficacy of proactive treatment of problem behavior. In W. Sailor, G. Dunlap, G. Sugai, & R. H. Horner (Eds.), *Handbook of positive behavior support* (pp. 107-123). New York: Springer.

Sugai, G., Horner, R. H., Dunlap, G., Hieneman, M., Lewis, T. J., Nelson, C. M., et al. (2000). Applying positive behavior support and functional behavioral assessment in schools. *Journal of Positive Behavior Interventions, 2,* 131-143.

Walker, H. M., Horner, R. H., Sugai, G., Bullis, M., Sprague, J. R., Bricker, D., et al. (1996). Integrated approaches to preventing antisocial behavior patterns among school-age children and youth. *Journal of Emotional and Behavioral Disorders, 4,* 194-209.

# Social Development and Intervention in Young Children With Autism Spectrum Disorders

**Kathy Lawton, Ph.D.,**

**Connie Kasari, Ph.D.,**
University of California, Los Angeles

Social impairment is a defining characteristic of autism spectrum disorders (ASDs). Regardless of an individual's age or ability level, social challenges are nearly always present. The difficulties are first noticed by family members and then later affect relationships with peers. In this article we describe two areas of concern that are among the first to emerge in young children with ASDs and strategies to promote positive social functioning in each area, joint attention and play.

## Early Social Skills

### Joint Attention Gestures

Before young children talk, they communicate with gestures. These early gestures have different functions. Some serve to request that a person do something (e.g., child points to request a drink in the refrigerator). Others are merely intended to share interest in an event or object with another person (e.g., child points at a cute puppy to share excitement about the puppy). This latter form of communication in which a child conveys pleasure or interest about an object, person, or event is called joint attention. Joint attention gestures of pointing, showing, giving, and looking serve a pivotal role in the development of communication and social skills. Children with ASDs, however, use a smaller quantity and a poorer quality of joint attention gestures (Kasari, Sigman, Mundy, & Yirmiya, 1990; Mundy, Sigman, Ungerer, & Sherman, 1986).

## Play

In this article we conceptualize play as the manipulation of objects as intended or in a pretend fashion. These types of play are called functional or symbolic. When engaging in functional play, children use objects as they are meant to be used (e.g., opening and closing a pop-up). In contrast, during symbolic play, children use objects with pretense (e.g., child pretends that a block is piece of food). Within these two broad categories, there are specific types of play that build upon each other. Table 1 lists these specific play "levels" as adapted from previous developmental sequencing of play (Lifter, Sulzer-Azaroff, Anderson, & Cowdery, 1993).

*Joint attention gestures of pointing, showing, giving, and looking serve a pivotal role in the development of communication and social skills.*

Functional and symbolic play skills help children engage in representational thinking, social interactions, and communication (Mundy, Sigman, Ungerer, & Sherman, 1987). Unfortunately, children with ASDs use less symbolic play than children who are typically developing and their sym-

Table 1
**Functional and Symbolic Play Levels[a]**

| Level of Play | Definition of Level | Examples |
|---|---|---|
| Level 1: Simple play | Single actions on objects | Rolls round beads |
| Level 2: Combinations | • Putting objects together<br>• Taking objects apart | • Takes all pieces out of puzzle<br>• Puts puzzle pieces into puzzle<br>• Stacks nesting cups<br>• Places cup on saucer |
| Level 3: Almost symbolic | • Relates objects to self, indicating a pretend quality to the action<br>• Extends familiar actions to doll figures, with the child as agent of the activity | • Brings empty cup to mouth to drink<br>• Extends cup to doll's mouth |
| Level 4: Symbolic | • Uses one object to stand in place for another<br>• Moves doll figures as if they are capable of action | • Puts bowl on head for a hat<br>• Moves figure to load blocks in a truck |

[a]This table is adapted from a publication by Kasari et al. (2006). These play levels are based upon the work of Lifter et al. (1993).

bolic play is of a lower quality than that of children who are typically developing (Hobson, Lee, & Hobson, 2009; Sigman & Ungerer, 1984).

Children with ASDs show a characteristic pattern of strengths and weaknesses in nonverbal communication gestures and play. Children with ASDs show more strengths in requesting gestures and functional play than joint attention gestures and symbolic play. Of particular importance is the association of these early developing impairments with later communication and social skills. Therefore, it should make sense why researchers "widely agree" that joint attention and play should be a focus of early intervention (Charman et al., 2003; Kasari, 2002).

## Interventions

In the past 10 years, researchers have developed several interventions for promoting the joint attention and play skills of children with ASDs. Many of these interventions report success in targeted skills such as joint attention, functional play, and symbolic play (e.g., Kasari, Freeman, & Paparella, 2006). In addition, a few joint attention and play intervention studies report benefits to skills, such as emotion regulation, that were not directly targeted in the intervention (e.g., Gulsrud, Jahromi, & Kasari, 2010).

### Active Ingredients of Intervention

Although some intervention studies report success at improving the joint attention and/or play of young children with autism, not all joint attention and/or play intervention studies do. There are several "active ingredients" or factors that appear to influence how successful a joint attention and/or play intervention will be: dose (how much of an intervention a child receives), content (what is taught), timing (when in development the skill is taught), and methodology (how the skill is taught; Kasari et al., 2005). In this article we briefly describe the methodology that appears to be most powerful for improving the joint attention and/or play skills of children with autism.

### Joint Engagement

Early intervention service providers and families should promote joint attention and/or play skills during periods of joint engagement. Joint engagement is a period of time in which children and adults are actively involved with the same object or activities (Adamson, Bakeman, & Deckner, 2004). Teaching the particular skill during joint engagement may lead to better language and help ensure that the targeted skill has meaning to the child. Supporting the child in joint engagement allows the child and adult to have a "topic" in which the child can learn the meaning of gestures and words. As such, longer periods of joint engagement are found to significantly predict later language use (Adamson, Bakeman, Deckner, & Romski, 2009). Additionally, if intervening during joint engagement, the child can learn how to use the targeted skill in context similar to how he or she would typically be expected to use the skill.

> *Supporting the child in joint engagement allows the child and adult to have a "topic" in which the child can learn the meaning of gestures and words.*

## Following the Child's Attentional Focus

Joint engagement may be established following either the adult or child's attentional focus. The term attentional focus refers to objects or activities that an individual is looking at for 3 or more seconds (Tomasello & Farrar, 1986). Another methodological active ingredient may be teaching a particular objective while following the child's attentional focus. If an adult is following the child's attentional focus, he or she will use objects the child selects and will try to maintain and join the child's attentional focus.

## Child Selection of Materials

The child will be motivated to engage in more instances of the targeted objective if the adult allows the child to select the objects that will be used during the interaction (e.g., Koegel, Dyer, & Bell, 1987). Sometimes children may indicate their preference for a particular object through words or gestures ("I want blocks" or pointing at the blocks). Other times children may show what object(s) they want to use by simply looking at the object (e.g., looking at a puzzle rather than the shape sorter).

## Shared Attention While Manipulating Objects

Another important way to follow the child's attentional focus is to establish and sustain "mutual understanding" to the object selected by the child (Pan, Imbens-Bailey, Winner, & Snow, 1996). The adult places only a small attentional burden on the child if he or she maintains and joins the child's focus of attention with the object the child selected. To maintain and follow a child's focus of attention, an adult must first "co-orient" (look) to the object at which the child is looking (Collis & Schaffer, 1978). The adult must continue to co-orient to the child-selected object throughout the interaction. The adult will be more likely to catch the child's attention and establish shared play if he or she gets down to the child's eye level and engages with the child-selected object in a way similar to the child's play with the object. For example, if a child is looking at a pretend apple, the adult must first notice how the child is using the pretend apple. The adult should then ensure that any play act he or she makes is referenced to the pretend apple because that is where the child's attention is focused. It is best for the adult to get down to the child's eye level and *imitate the child's play action.* However, if the child is not performing a play act with the pretend apple, the adult could *model a play act* using the pretend apple.

> *The adult will be more likely to catch the child's attention and establish shared play if he or she gets down to the child's eye level and engages with the child-selected object in a way similar to the child's play with the object.*

Using child-selected objects outside of the child's attentional focus will intensify the difficulty of interactions that we already know are quite challenging for children with ASDs. If an adult redirects a child's attention to objects outside of his or her attentional focus, a larger cognitive burden will be placed on the child (Landry & Chapieski, 1989). Suppose again that a child is pretending to eat a watermelon slice. An adult is redirecting the child's attentional focus if he or she gets out a plate the child is not looking at and instructs the child to put his or her watermelon slice on the plate.

## Developmentally Appropriate, Individualized Intervention Objectives

An adult will need to target a developmentally appropriate, individualized intervention objective while following the child's attentional focus during joint engagement. Even if an intervention is targeting a common goal across all children with ASDs (e.g., more instances of joint attention), an intervention will most likely be more successful if specific intervention objectives are modified to the unique profile of the child receiving the intervention. The presentation of ASDs varies greatly between individuals, so the same intervention will not work in the same way for all children with ASDs (National Research Council, 2001). Therefore, one potential active ingredient is individualized, developmentally appropriate intervention targets.

**Developmentally Appropriate Targets of Intervention**. Adults should pinpoint developmentally appropriate intervention objectives for each child. As previously explained, nonverbal communication and play are comprised of a hierarchy of skills or levels. For example, we have already noted that play is composed of functional and symbolic play that progresses in complexity. If an adult teaches a joint attention or play intervention objective that emerges next in a child's development, intervention efficacy can be maximized.

Some joint attention and play interventions have taught children specific skills in the order that the skill emerges in typical development with some modifications for the unique profile of ASDs. An intervention by Kasari et al. (2006) is one such example. The order with which specific joint attention and play objectives were taught was based upon past literature regarding the developmental emergence of each skill and the ease with which this skill could be achieved in children with ASDs.

Kasari et al. (2006) also selected the intervention target based on the child's existing skill set. Some interventions teach skills in a "standard" or invariant order regardless of what the child can already do. Teaching intervention objectives in an invariant order may have some disadvantages. In some cases, the child may already know the taught skill(s). Another notable disadvantage is that some of the target skills may be too far out of the child's reach.

**Using Assessment to Create Individualized Intervention Objectives.** How do you know what skill to begin with? In the case of ASDs, one should first teach a skill that the child does not demonstrate solidly and then target a skill that should emerge next in the child's development (Kasari, Gulsrud, Wong, Kwon, & Locke, 2010). Teaching a skill that is within the child's reach will help ensure that the interaction is not too challenging for the child and that the child is developmentally "ready" to understand the true meaning of the skill.

Selecting developmentally appropriate target(s) of intervention will be best accomplished through assessment. Prior to starting an intervention, one should assess the child's competency with a particular intervention target (Sandall, Hemmeter, Smith, & McLean, 2005). There are several ways that one can assess a child's fluency in joint attention or play at the beginning and end of an intervention. All skills can be informally assessed through observations of the child during naturally occurring interactions (e.g., Schertz & Odom, 2007). For example, an adult can watch a child as the child plays with peers or an adult. The adult can note whether the

child is using joint attention and at what level of
play the child is using
toys. Adults can also
use semistandardized
assessments designed to
measure joint attention
(e.g., The Early Social
Communication Scales;
Mundy et al., 2003) or
play (e.g., The Structured
Play Assessment; Ungerer
& Sigman, 1981).

Throughout the intervention, one should monitor how the child is acquiring a particular objective and make any necessary adjustments to the goal (Sandall et al., 2005). Adults should decide ahead of time what level of performance will indicate mastery of a particular skill. Often mastery is determined by specifying how often a child needs to display a certain level of the skill over a specific amount of time (Alberto & Troutman, 2005). For example, Whalen and Schreibman (2003) stipulated ahead of time that a specific joint attention target would be deemed mastered if the child responded to 80% of opportunities over the course of four to five consecutive sessions. Once the intervention objective is selected, the adult should use ongoing assessment to monitor how the child is acquiring a particular objective. A child's performance could be monitored by collecting data during each session (e.g., Whalen & Schriebman, 2003).

## Conclusions

Interventions that include the following strategies may have more success at teaching joint attention and/or play than interventions that do not include these strategies: joint engagement; following the child's attentional focus; and individualized, developmentally appropriate intervention targets. These strategies may be a few active ingredients for inducing favorable treatment-related gains in joint attention and play (e.g., Kasari et al., 2006). Given that these strategies seem to be active ingredients in interventions for joint attention and play, we encourage practitioners and parents to consider using these strategies in order to improve the social impairments of joint attention and play in young children with ASDs. Bringing strategies used in research studies into the practice arena is important if we are to bridge the research to practice gap.

Very few intervention studies that target joint attention and/or play are conducted in applied settings. Therefore, we recommend that researchers consider the application of interventions in real-world contexts, such as homes or schools. Schools may be an especially important context for teaching these skills because the number of preschoolers with ASDs attending public preschools is increasing (e.g., Bitterman, Daley, Misra, Carlson, & Markowitz, 2008). Additionally, research suggests that public preschools are challenged in optimizing the social communication of preschoolers with ASDs (e.g., Hess, Morrier, Heflin, & Ivey, 2008).

In summary, there are currently several examples of efficacious interventions with promising findings of improved social communication outcomes for young children with ASDs. A number of strategies were identified that are likely active ingredients of effective joint attention and play interventions. The application of the proposed strategies may facilitate better social communication outcomes in young children with ASDs.

## Note

Correspondence concerning this article may be e-mailed to Connie Kasari at Kasari@gseis.ucla.edu

The development of this chapter was supported by the Autism Intervention Research-Network funded by U.S. Department of Health and Human Services HRSA, Maternal and Child Health Branch Grant #UA3MC11055, NIH RO1 MH 084864; Project 4 of 5P50HD055784, Autism Speaks Characterizing Cognition in Nonverbal Children with Autism; and the ACE Center grant: NIH/NICHD #P50-HD-055784, all awarded to Connie Kasari.

## References

Adamson, L. B., Bakeman, R., & Deckner, D. F. (2004). The development of symbol-infused joint engagement. *Child Development, 75,* 1171-1187.

Adamson, L. B., Bakeman, R., Deckner, D. F., & Romski, M. (2009). Joint engagement and the emergence of language in children with autism and Down syndrome. *Journal of Autism and Developmental Disorders, 39,* 84-96.

Alberto, P. A. & Troutman, A. C. (2005). *Applied behavior analysis for teachers.* Columbus, OH: Pearson Merrill Prentice Hall.

Bitterman, A., Daley, T. C., Misra, S., Carlson, E., & Markowitz, J. (2008). A national sample of preschoolers with autism spectrum disorders: Special education services and parent satisfaction. *Journal of Autism and Developmental Disorders, 38,* 1509-1517.

Charman, T., Baron-Cohen, S., Swettenham, J., Baird, G., Drew, A., & Cox, A. (2003). Predicting language outcome in infants with ASD and pervasive developmental disorder. *International Journal of Language and Communication Disorders, 38,* 265-285.

Collis, G. M. & Schaffer, H. R. (1978). Synchronization of visual attention in mother-infant pairs. *Journal of Child Psychology and Psychiatry, 16,* 315-320.

Gulsrud, A. C., Jahromi, L. B, & Kasari, C. (2010). The co-regulation of emotions between mothers and their children with ASD. *Journal of ASD and Developmental Disorders, 40, 227-237.*

Hess, K. L., Morrier, M. J., Heflin, J., & Ivey, M. L. (2008). Autism treatment survey: Services by children with autism spectrum disorders in public school classrooms. *Journal of Autism and Developmental Disorders, 38,* 961-971.

Hobson, P. R., Lee, A., & Hobson, J. A. (2009). Qualities of symbolic play among children with ASD: A social-developmental perspective. *Journal of ASD and Developmental Disorders, 39,* 12-22.

Kasari, C. (2002). Assessing change in early intervention programs for children with autism. *Journal of Autism and Developmental Disorders, 32,* 447-461.

Kasari, C., Freeman, S., & Paparella, T. (2006). Joint attention and symbolic play in children with ASD: A randomized control joint attention intervention. *Journal of Child Psychology and Psychiatry, 47,* 611-620.

Kasari, C., Freeman, S., Paparella, T., Wong, C., Kwon, S., & Gulsrud, A. (2005). Early intervention on core deficits in ASD. *Clinical Neuropsychiatry, 2,* 380-388.

Kasari, C., Gulsrud, A. C., Wong, C., Kwon, S., & Locke, J. (2010). Randomized controlled caregiver mediated joint engagement intervention for toddlers with ASD. *Journal of ASD and Developmental Disorders, 40*(9), 1045-1056.

Kasari, C., Sigman, M., Mundy, P., & Yirmiya, N. (1990). Affective sharing in the context of joint attention interactions of normal, autistic, and mentally retarded children. *Journal of Autism and Developmental Disorders, 20,* 87-100.

Koegel, R. L., Dyer, K., & Bell, L. K. (1987). The influence of child-preferred activities on autistic children's social behaviors. *Journal of Applied Behavior Analysis, 20,* 243-252.

Landry, S. H. & Chapieski, M. L. (1989). Joint attention and infant toy exploration: Effects of down syndrome and prematurity. *Child Development, 60,* 103-118.

Lifter, K., Sulzer-Azaroff, B., Anderson, S., & Cowdery, G. E. (1993). Teaching play activities to preschool children with disabilities: The importance of developmental considerations. *Journal of Early Intervention, 17,* 139–159.

Mundy, P., Delgado, C., Block, J., Venezia, M., Hogan, A., & Seibert, J. (2003). *A manual for the abridged Early Social Communication Scales (ESCS).* Unpublished manuscript, University of Miami.

Mundy, P., Sigman, M., Ungerer, J., & Sherman, T. (1986). Defining the social deficits of ASD: The contribution of non-verbal communication measures. *Journal of Child Psychiatry, 27,* 657-669.

Mundy, P., Sigman, M., Ungerer, J., & Sherman, T. (1987). Nonverbal communication and play correlates of language development in autistic children. *Journal of ASD and Developmental Disorders, 17,* 349-364.

National Research Council. (2001). *Educating children with autism.* Washington, DC: National Academy Press.

Pan, B. A., Imbens-Bailey, A., Winner, K., & Snow, C. (1996). Communicative intents expressed by parents in interaction with young children. *Merrill-Palmer Quarterly, 42,* 248-267.

Sandall, S., Hemmeter, M. L., Smith, B., & McLean, M. (2005). *DEC recommended practices: A comprehensive guide for practical application in early intervention/early childhood special education.* Longmont, CO: Sopris West.

Schertz, H. H. & Odom, S. L. (2007). Promoting joint attention in toddlers with ASD: A parent-mediated developmental model. *Journal of ASD and Developmental Disabilities, 37,* 1562-1575.

Sigman, M. & Ungerer, J. A. (1984). Cognitive and language skills in autistic, mentally retarded, and normal children. *Developmental Psychology, 20,* 293-302.

Tomasello, M. & Farrar, M. J. (1986). Joint attention and early language. *Child Development, 57,* 1454-1463.

Ungerer, J. A. & Sigman, M. (1981). Symbolic play and language comprehension in autistic children. *American Academy of Child Psychiatry, 20,* 318-337.

Whalen, C. & Schreibman, L (2003). Joint attention training for children with ASD using behavior modification procedures. *Journal of Child Psychology and Psychiatry, 44,* 456-468.

# Initial Inclusion of 2- and 3-Year-Old Children With Autism Spectrum Disorders

## Planning for and Surviving the First Few Days

**Mark Wolery, Ph.D.,**
Vanderbilt University

**Ann N. Garfinkle, Ph.D.,**
University of Montana

**J**eremy *is 26 months old and was given a diagnosis of autism last month. He is the only child of Virginia (a stay-at-home mother and former third-grade teacher) and Ray (a manager of a fast food restaurant). They have the option of placing him in a full-day, inclusive childcare program. Virginia had planned to go back to work when Jeremy went to kindergarten, but she misses teaching and the extra income would be helpful. They, however, are hesitant about putting Jeremy in the program. What if it does not work out, what if he gets kicked out, what if it is too hard on him? Jeremy has never been in group care and, in fact, has never spent more than an hour or two away from one of his parents. How can he possibly be included in a full-day program? Can the staff of the program do anything to increase the chances such a placement would be successful for Jeremy as well as for his parents?*

The rationale for inclusive early education was articulated many years ago (Bricker, 1978). Barriers to, and supports for, high-quality inclusive early education are known (Odom, 2002) as are procedures for teaching children with disabilities in inclusive classes (McWilliam, Wolery, & Odom, 2002; Wolery & Wilbers, 1994). Model inclusive programs exist for children with nearly all types of disabilities (Guralnick, 2002), including young children with autism (Strain, McGee, & Kohler, 2002). Guidelines for inclusion exist for administrators (Strain, Wolery, & Izeman, 1998). The models and characteristics of effective early education programs for young children with autism also have been demonstrated and evaluated

(Dawson & Osterling, 1997; National Research Council, 2001). Inclusive classes provide children with autism competent interactive and communicative partners, models of prosocial and adaptive behavior, and normalized early group care experiences. The purpose of this article is to describe a set of recommendations for the *initial* inclusion of 2- and 3-year-old children with autism in early education classrooms. The recommendations are based on experience and, for the most part, on research findings. They are divided into two categories: planning for the child's enrollment, and practices to use from the first day. In making these recommendations, we assume the classroom into which the child is placed is equipped and staffed adequately; is of high quality for children without disabilities; and has access to expertise, training, and assistance for the classroom staff on a continual basis. Many important issues are not discussed in this article, such as establishing an intervention team, coordinating related therapy services, supporting families and siblings, assisting families in making decisions about alternative treatments, and planning transitions across service systems (i.e., from Part C to preschool services).

## Planning to Enroll a Young Child With Autism

The enrollment of any young child into group care is important and deserves careful planning; however, this is particularly true if the child has an autism spectrum disorder. While the placement decision resides with the individualized family service plan or the individualized education program team, the decision ultimately rests with the family. They can choose whether to enroll their child.

### Have the Parents and Child Visit the Target Classroom Before Actual Enrollment

This visit has several purposes, such as letting the parents and classroom staff meet one another, allowing the parents to evaluate the class, and giving parents an opportunity to make judgments about how caring and accepting the classroom staff are of their child and of them. The visit also allows the child to "scope out" the classroom and allows the staff to identify toys and classroom areas to which the child naturally gravitates. This is useful in identifying the child's potential interests and toys to which the child may be attracted. Ideally, this visit would begin about the time the class is finishing an engaging activity and transitioning to outdoor play. The child with autism and his parents accompanied by a professional can remain in the classroom after the children and teacher go to the playground. By remaining in the classroom, the child has a nonthreatening time to explore the classroom and materials. Subsequently, joining the class on the playground is useful, because the child can run about the playground and the parents can speak with staff and watch the other children.

## Plan the Daily Separation With the Family

A flexible separation policy is ideal. Many parents of 2- and 3-year-old children with autism have never left their child in group care; thus, this can be a frightening experience and calls for planning how it will be done. As the child's attendance continues, the most useful separation practice is for the child and parent to enter the class, be greeted by classroom staff and other children, and then have a "good-bye" routine established between the child and parent. However, for the first few days, flexibility is needed to ensure the comfort of both the child and the parents. Parents vary greatly on their desires about how to separate; some want to transfer the child quickly to another adult and then be alone with their own thoughts and emotions. Others may want to (1) sneak out as the child becomes engaged, (2) prolong the good-bye, or (3) remain and observe. One should present options to the family before the first day, let them choose, and assure them staff will support their choice. Further, families should be assured the classroom staff is competent in handling children's separation from their parents. However, despite having agreed to a separation practice for the first few days, the staff should adapt if families change their minds and do something other than what was planned.

*Comfort items are useful for helping the child learn to regulate himself or herself in the classroom . . . and for helping him or her through difficult events in the classroom.*

## Get Information About the Child Before He or She Attends

In addition to the usual assessments and enrollment information regarding medical needs, allergies, special diets, and emergency contacts, several other types of information are critical. Families are a source of important information, and they often are willing to share it if asked. One should identify any objects (pacifier, blanket, toy, etc.) that appear to calm or comfort the child ("comfort items"). Comfort items are useful for helping the child learn to regulate himself or herself in the classroom. Such objects are often useful in calming children and helping them through difficult events in the classroom. One should identify the foods and drinks the child prefers and ensure those are available during snack and meals. The staff should identify the child's interests in terms of toys, songs, books, and routines. These should be embedded into other activities to entice the child's engagement and to extend it. For example, if the child is interested in trains, one should have a train set available with which the child can play when he or she enters the classroom and use trains in the art and circle time activities. The staff should find out how the child communicates wants and needs and identify any familiar play routines the child has with his or her family (e.g., does the child play patty cake or some individually devised game). For example, one child liked to count things, and counting steps or objects helped him manage initial classroom transitions and activities. Finally, one should identify any aversive stimuli or activities and avoid them during initial enrollment. For example, if the child avoids touching messy materials, the art activities should be something other than finger painting for the first week or two. This information, of course, must be shared with the classroom staff.

## Be Open to Using a Phased-in Attendance Approach

Ideally, children would attend each day for the full day the class is in operation (e.g., all day for full-day childcare, half-days if the program is a half-day program). However, over the first couple of weeks, the number of hours of attendance can be increased gradually. The primary rationale for phased-in attendance is to maximize the likelihood the experience is positive for the child. For example, the child could attend for 2 hours for the first 3 days and then 3 the next couple of days, and so forth. Within 2 or 3 weeks, the child would ideally be attending full-time. During those first few days, the child should attend when the activities in which he or she is most likely to be interested are occurring. For some children, phased-in attendance is not practical because their families must be at work or transportation is impossible to arrange. However, we have found it useful when it is feasible.

## Have an Extra Person With Expertise Available During the First Few Days

This person should know the child and family and should be familiar with the children and staff in the classroom. This person must have expertise in working effectively with young children with autism and may be a special educator or a related service staff member who works with the child. Ideally, the person would be available to talk with the family and interpret what is occurring if the family is observing. This person also can step in and help the classroom staff adjust to having a new child in the class and can help make on-the-spot decisions related to the child and the classroom activities. This expert can help minimize the disruptions that might be caused by adding a new child and can provide training to the classroom staff about how to include the child. Finally, this extra staff member can record some videotape to share with the child's family. Although the recommendation to have an expert available may seem unrealistic, ongoing access to expertise is necessary if young children with autism are to be included successfully. Having such expertise available during the first critical days prevents problems and communicates support to the staff and the family.

## First Day Practices

The previous recommendations focus on planning for the enrollment of a young child with autism in an inclusive classroom. We have found the following practices should be in place from the first day of enrollment. These practices should help build success from the beginning.

### Communicate With the Family on the Child's First Day of Enrollment

Although communication with families should occur before and after enrollment, this recommendation speaks to the first day of the child's attendance. For families who remain and observe the class (ideally from outside the classroom), one should be sure a knowledgeable professional can be with them and help interpret what is occurring, explain why given practices are being used, and answer questions they may have. For families who leave the center or school, phone numbers should be exchanged with them. One should assure them it is okay to call and check and get their permission to call them during the day to give them a report. In such calls, one should report on the positive things the child is doing and assure the parents the child will do well. If the family transports the child, someone must be at the class and free to talk with them at both the drop off and pick up times. For all families (those who stay and observe and those who do not), the staff should make a video for them of the child's first day and give it to them at the end of the day. Care should be taken to

*For families who leave the classroom, their last image may be of the child upset and crying; seeing a video with the child enjoying and participating in an activity is reassuring that the child did not spend the entire day upset*

ensure only children with video releases are included. This video should be a fair representation of the child's day—times when things go well and not so well. By showing both extremes, the family can assess how the child is doing and how the staff is interacting with their child. For families who leave the classroom, their last image may be of the child upset and crying; seeing the video with the child enjoying and participating in an activity is reassuring that the child did not spend the entire day upset. In addition, the videotape can be used to show other family members who do not see the child in the class. When things are not going well, one should solicit suggestions from the family. They may well have notions about how to assist the child in the classroom.

## Operate the Classroom Activities as Usual and Follow the Complete Schedule

The usual schedule of activities and routines should be used from the first day. The goal is to assist the child in following the daily events; this, of course, requires planning. Some modifications of the nature of activities in any given block may be needed; for example, if there is a regular time for engaging in sensory experiences, the specific materials should be selected based on the child's interests, but such activities should occur as scheduled. Planning field trips and outings during the child's first couple weeks of enrollment is not advised, but including the child in subsequent field trips and excursions is strongly recommended. Class field trips with adequate adult supervision are important in helping children learn to negotiate community settings. As with the schedule, we have found classroom displays (e.g., pictures, art work) should not be taken away. The staff should arrange, decorate, and schedule the classroom in keeping with practices recommended for high-quality early childhood programs.

## Use Visual Cues to Assist the Child in Transitions and Activities

Transitions between activities tend to be unsuccessful for young children with autism, in part, because they may not be able to predict or understand *where* they are supposed to be, *what* they are supposed to do, and *when* they will be finished with it. Providing them with visual cues from the first day assists in communicating what is expected and coming next. Although pictures can be used, three-dimensional objects are often more useful for young children. Examples include disposable diapers to transition to the changing table, a plastic soap container to transition to hand washing, a puzzle piece to transition to a table to work puzzles, a shovel from the sand box to transition to the playground, a paintbrush to transition to an art activity, and a block to transition to the block area. Initially, adults can pair the visual cues with verbal directions and physical guidance, fading the physical prompts over time through graduated guidance (Bryan & Gast, 2000). The visual cues also can be faded as the child begins to use naturally occurring cues (e.g., peers lining up to wash their hands) as a cue to the nature of the transition. Using visual cues such as carpet squares can assist the child in knowing where to be during times when children are sitting on the floor (e.g., at circle time) and footprints near the sink where children may stand in line are recommended. Having the child's picture on the table communicates the child's place at the table.

## Ensure All Classroom Staff Have Pleasant Interactions With the Child Each Day

Some young children with autism who are enrolled in inclusive classes appear to "latch" on to one of the adults in the class. We want to promote strong positive relationships between children and their teachers, but those relationships need to be with all the classroom staff not a single adult. As a result, from the first day of enrollment, all adults who work in the class (teachers, assistants, specialists) should have several pleasant interactions with the child each day. These interactions occur by following the child's lead, responding positively to the child's behavior, giving the child objects he or she desires, playing interactive games (e.g., patty cake), singing favorite songs, looking at favorite books, and so forth. The point is to help the child be comfortable and engaged regardless of which adults are present.

## Embed Preferred Toys and Materials Into Other Activities

Although by definition young children with autism have restricted interests, most approach some toys or materials more readily than others. Families often have information about which toys and materials attract their child's attention and engagement. These toys should be made a part of existing activities.

## Provide Frequent Choices of Toys and Materials

High-quality early education programs for typically developing children use a child-centered, play-based curriculum, which involves frequent child choices of materials and activity areas. Although some young children with autism cannot indicate their choices through verbal requests or verbal answers, they often can make nonverbal selections between one toy and another. From the first day, children should be given many explicit choices each day; the use of antecedent choice is associated with increases in engagement and decreases in problematic behaviors (Reinhartsen, Garfinkle, & Wolery, 2003). For example, when the child is unengaged, the adult can hold two toys (e.g., truck and pop bead) in front of the child and look expectantly at the child. If the child reaches for one of the toys, the adult should give him or her the toy and help the child play with it. Providing frequent choices from the beginning allows the child some autonomy and control over the classroom environment.

## Minimize the Child's Waiting During Classroom Activities

*Minimizing waiting is particularly important during the first days of enrollment for young children with autism. Thus, during the first few days of enrollment, one should be sure the next area is available before starting the transition of the child to the next activity or routine.*

Waiting in line for a turn or for materials should be minimized for all children, but some waiting (e.g., to wash hands) is often inevitable. Minimizing waiting is particularly important during the first days of enrollment for young children with autism. Thus, during the first few days of enrollment, the staff should be sure the next area is available before starting the transition of the child to the next activity or routine. For example, when getting ready to change a diaper or to wash hands, one should be sure the changing area or sink is vacant. Likewise, before transitioning the child to circle time or to another activity, one should be sure there is a space available for the child and start the activity before or as the child arrives.

## Use Predictable Routines and Activities

Being able to predict what will happen next is important for all children; however, it appears to be particularly important for young children with autism. Thus, from the first day, the staff should have a defined schedule of activities (i.e., the usual class schedule), but within those activities one should build in predictable routines. For example, during circle time there should be a prescribed sequence of activities. If it involves singing songs, one should embed turn-taking into those songs, provide visual choices (e.g., with cards depicting songs), and have consistent transition routines between activities. Similarly, during free play the staff should embed social game playing such as "ring-around-the-rosy" and "row-row-

row your boat," which have defined sets of actions tied to given portions of the routines. The predictability of such social routines minimizes the uncertainty involved in new situations and provides plentiful opportunities for social contact with positive adults and proximity with peers.

## Avoid Unnecessary Battles With the Child

As with many of the recommendations noted previously, skilled teachers avoid battles with all 2- and 3-year-old children; this practice is especially important with young children who have autism. A primary

goal of the first couple weeks of enrollment in an inclusive class is to assist the child in learning to manage the classroom routines and schedules with ease and without tantrums and "melt downs." Activities that are likely to result in such behavior should be adapted by allowing the child to escape (appropriately) and withdraw from the hustle and bustle of the classroom, regroup, and then reenter the activity. Before allowing the child to escape an activity, the staff should ensure a simple desirable behavior occurs before allowing the child to withdraw. Allowing the child access to comfort toys or objects is relevant at such times. These times should be relatively brief (a few minutes), but they are often necessary. Also, during the initial enrollment, one should avoid putting extra demands on the child. This is not to imply the child is allowed total free rein, of course not, because that would teach undesirable behavioral patterns. However, expecting behaviors for which children are currently proficient as compared to those they are just starting to learn is important during initial enrollment.

## Use Rich Schedules of Reinforcement (Rewards)

During the initial enrollment, children should receive frequent reinforcement for adaptive behavior, for staying in activities, for being near other children, and for following classroom routines. For many young children with autism, the stimuli that will function as powerful positive reinforcers may be limited in number. Thus, identifying powerful and deliverable reinforcers for young children with autism requires expertise. Often a powerful reinforcer for young children with autism is time alone away from other children and from demands. Similarly, objects used in stereotypic behavior often have reinforcing power. Unfortunately, these reinforcers can be difficult to deliver contingently and they may interfere with ongoing engagement with materials and interactions with others. However, to establish adaptive behavior and to maintain appropriate behavior in new classroom situations, frequent reinforcement is necessary.

In this article, five general recommendations for planning the initial placement of 2- or 3-year old children with autism are discussed. Further, 10 practices to use from the first day of enrollment were described. These recommendations are listed in Table 1. All of the suggestions, of course, are only relevant if the classroom is of high quality (e.g., carries accreditation from the National Association for the Education of Young Children), if the teaching staff has some advance training and are skilled in interacting with young children in general, and if the teaching staff have ready access to individuals who have expertise in autism and inclusive early education. These recommendations are presented to

Table 1
**Planning for Initial Inclusion of Young Children With Autism**

| **Recommendations for Planning Prior to Enrollment** |
| --- |
| Have the parents and child visit the classroom before actual attendance |
| Discuss with the family and agree on how the daily separation will occur |
| Get information about the child before he or she attends |
| Be open to the possibility of using a phased-in attendance |
| Have an extra person with expertise available during the first few days |
| **Recommended Practices for the First Day(s)** |
| During the child's first day of enrollment, communicate with the family |
| Operate the classroom activities as usual and follow the complete schedule |
| Use visual cues to assist the child in transitions and activities |
| Ensure all classroom staff have pleasant interactions with the child each day |
| Embed preferred toys and materials into other activities |
| Provide frequent choices of toys and materials |
| Minimize the child's waiting during classroom activities |
| Use predictable routines and activities |
| Avoid unnecessary battles with the child |
| Use rich schedules of reinforcement (rewards) |

increase opportunities for young children with autism to be included in classrooms with their typically developing peers. Once included, other practice recommendations must be used to ensure they learn from those experiences.

## Note

The authors may be contacted by e-mail at mark.wolery@vanderbilt.edu or Ann.Garfinkle@mso.umt.edu

## References

Bricker, D. D. (1978). A rationale for the integration of handicapped and nonhandicapped preschool children. In M. J. Guralnick (Ed.), *Early intervention and the integration of handicapped and nonhandicapped children* (pp. 3-26). Baltimore: University Park Press.

Bryan, L. C. & Gast, D. L. (2000). Teaching on-task and on-schedule behaviors to high-functioning children with autism via picture activity schedules. *Journal of Autism and Developmental Disorders, 30,* 553-567.

Dawson, G. & Osterling, J. (1997). Early intervention in autism. In M. J. Grualnick (Ed.), *The effectiveness of early intervention* (pp. 307-326). Baltimore: Paul Brookes.

Guralnick, M. J. (2002). *Early childhood inclusion: Focus on change.* Baltimore: Paul Brookes.

McWilliam, R. A., Wolery, M., & Odom, S. L. (2002). Instructional perspectives in inclusive preschool classrooms. In M. J. Guralnick (Ed.), *Early childhood inclusion: Focus on change* (pp. 503-527). Baltimore: Paul Brookes.

National Research Council. (2001). *Educating children with autism.* Washington, DC: National Academy of Science.

Odom, S. L. (2002). *Widening the circle: Including children with disabilities in preschool programs.* New York: Teachers College Press.

Reinhartsen, D. R., Garfinkle, A. N., & Wolery, M. (2002). Engagement with toys in two-year-old children with autism: Teacher selection and child choice. *Research and Practice for Persons with Severe Disabilities, 27,* 175-187.

Strain, P. S., McGee, G. G., & Kohler, F. W. (2002). Inclusion of children with autism in early intervention environments. In M. J. Guralnick (Ed.), *Early childhood inclusion: Focus on change* (pp. 337-363). Baltimore: Paul Brookes.

Strain, P. S., Wolery, M., & Izeman, S. (1998). Considerations for administrators in the design of service options for young children with autism and their families. *Young Exceptional Children, 1,* 1-16.

Wolery, M. & Wilbers, J. S. (1994). *Including children with special needs in early childhood programs.* Washington, DC: National Association for the Education of Young Children.

# Using Small Group Instruction to Teach Young Children With Autism Spectrum Disorders in Early Childhood Classes

Elizabeth A. Lewis, M.Ed.,

Jennifer R. Ledford, M.Ed.,

Katherine L. Elam, M.Ed.,

Mark Wolery, Ph.D.,
Vanderbilt University, Nashville, TN

David L. Gast, Ph.D.,
University of Georgia, Athens

Justin is a 4-year-old who attends an inclusive preschool program for children with autism spectrum disorders (ASD). He shows interest in his peers but often lacks the skills to interact with them appropriately. His teacher, Ms. Taylor, began the year using one-on-one direct instruction as her primary teaching tool for the students with ASD in her classroom. As the year progressed, she began to notice Justin was still not interacting with peers unless instructed to do so by an adult. She decided to change her instruction to see if she could encourage Justin to be more involved with his peers.

Ms. Taylor decided to teach Justin to count objects during small group center time rather than working on this objective individually. She had several typically developing students who were able to count objects but who struggled with identifying numerals. She decided to teach this related skill to two typically developing peers during a small group activity with Justin. She had Justin count items on a card and then had one of two peers find the numeral that corresponded to that number. Initially, small group was a challenge. Justin attempted to leave the table after a few minutes of working and often sang repetitively to *himself when it was not his turn. Ms. Taylor made some changes to the group, including using picture cues to let children know when it was their turn and planning short breaks during the session.*

*After a week of this routine, the children began demonstrating improved numeracy and social skills. Justin started watching his peers and giving them high fives when they chose the correct numeral! He sat for longer periods of time and started initiating to his peers by saying "Come on!" when the visual schedule in the classroom indicated that it was time for centers. During free play one morning, Ms. Taylor saw Justin and one of the peers from his small group looking at a book together and counting items on the pages. During calendar time, Justin and his peers worked together to correctly name the numbers on the calendar, and at snack time, the peers in Justin's small group began requesting to sit near him.*

Children with ASD often benefit from direct instruction, in which the teacher uses a systematic process for teaching and removing prompts and teaches specific behaviors until the children learn those skills (Reichow & Wolery, 2009). However, much of this instruction has occurred in a one-to-one arrangement, which is difficult to do in many classrooms. In this article, we describe small group instruction, a process for directly teaching specific skills to more than one child at a time. In the subsequent sections, we describe reasons for using small group instruction, variations that can occur, and recommendations for teachers.

## Rationale for Small Group Direct Instruction

Many children with ASD who receive individual (one-to-one) instruction on specific objectives in early childhood classes experience limited opportunities to interact or learn from their peers. Individual instruction is more restrictive than a small group arrangement and may not prepare children for early elementary school classes, where group instruction is the primary teaching approach. In addition, one-to-one instruction requires significant teacher resources for implementation and planning. Furthermore, children who are not receiving individual instruction must be supervised and engaged in other activities, which often results in the need for higher child-to-teacher

*Individual instruction is more restrictive than a small group arrangement and may not prepare children for early elementary school classes, where group instruction is the primary teaching approach.*

ratios. Using direct instruction in small group arrangements allows teachers to teach skills to multiple children in a small, structured setting. It also allows children to take advantage of peer models and naturally occurring opportunities to learn important social classroom behaviors such as turn taking and attending to peers.

## Social Learning Opportunities

Social difficulties are a primary diagnostic characteristic for children with ASD; thus, many individualized education plan goals for children with ASD are social in nature. During unstructured activities, children with ASD may be isolated, even when sharing physical space with typical peers (Wolfberg et al., 1999), and there is some evidence that peers perceive students with disabilities as members of peer groups that include only other students with disabilities (Boutot & Bryant, 2005). Children with disabilities in early childhood classes are less socially engaged with their peers than are their typically developing peers (Odom et al., 2004). This suggests that including children in classrooms with typically developing peers does not, in itself, necessarily lead to high rates of social opportunities. Planned, systematic instruction may be needed to support engagement of some children with ASD in group activities and to teach complicated skills such as turn taking, watching peers, and imitating peers' behaviors.

Observational learning occurs when children learn new skills by watching or listening to others model those skills. Although the use of direct instruction is advised, the use of one-to-one instruction may be limiting because of restricted opportunities to teach social skills and to learn through observing others. Decreased opportunity for social engagement is a significant problem with one-to-one instruction because social deficits are a primary concern for children with ASD. However, small group instruction provides an opportunity to supply structured proximity for children with ASD, which can increase the likelihood that they will acquire appropriate social skills. Observational learning is likely to occur in small group instructional arrangements (Ledford, Gast, Luscre, & Ayres, 2008).

## Peer Relationships

Using strategies to minimize errors and increase the rate of learning (e.g., constant time delay; Wolery, 2001) may increase success for children with ASD and allow them to demonstrate competence in front of peers. This is important because perceived competence appears to be related to social acceptance ratings and willingness of peers to include children with disabilities in typical preschool activities (Diamond & Huifang, 2009). Thus, small group instruction might help children learn appropriate behaviors with indirect benefits on social participation by positively influencing peers' perceptions of children with ASD.

## Least Restrictive Environments

Children with ASD are more likely than children with other disabilities to be placed in more restrictive settings in preschool (Bitterman, Daley, Misra, Carlson, & Markowitz, 2008). They are 4 times more likely to be assigned an individual assistant and less likely to be placed in inclusive preschool classrooms (Bitterman et al., 2008). The presence of an assistant can lead to social isolation for children with ASD (Boutot & Bryant, 2005) and result in a more restrictive experience if the child is removed from activities with peers for individual instruction. However, using assistants to teach children with ASD in the context of a peer group (e.g., with two typically developing peers) may minimize these negative social effects.

In addition to providing social opportunities in preschool, small group instruction provided in early childhood programs may prepare children for inclusive classes in elementary school. Low on-task behavior and not participating in group activities have been reported for children with disabilities in elementary school (Kemp & Carter, 2006). In addition, needing one-to-one instruction and not learning during group instruction were often-cited reasons for placing children in more restrictive elementary classes after attending inclusive preschools (Hanson et al., 2001). Thus, developmentally appropriate small group instruction can provide children with opportunities to develop group participation skills needed for successful inclusion in general education environments in elementary school.

*Small group instruction provides an opportunity to supply structured proximity for children with ASD, which can increase the likelihood that they will acquire appropriate social skills.*

## Practicality and Effectiveness

Another reason for using small group instead of one-to-one instruction is that it allows adults to supervise and teach more than one child at a time. This efficient use of adult time makes it possible to provide direct instruction to children who need it (most young children with ASD) in classrooms without enough adults to use one-to-one instruction. Small group instruction is not only practical but also effective (Ledford et al., 2008).

## Variations in Small Group Instruction

Teachers use many different methods to provide group instruction for young children. In one variation, three or four children take turns in a game of responding to the teacher. In another, children may work quietly at a table on a cooperative project. We are suggesting that small group arrangements be used to directly teach individualized behaviors, rather than simply ensuring that all children are in proximity and working with similar materials. This direct teaching can happen in a number of ways, and adding variety to small group instruction may help increase child respond-

Table 1
**Considerations for Planning Small Group Instruction**

| Planning Questions | Optional Arrangements or Activities | Advantages |
|---|---|---|
| Who should I include in my small group instruction? | • One child with autism spectrum disorders (ASD) and one or more typically developing peers<br>• Two children with ASD or one child with ASD and peers with other disabilities | • Children with ASD have opportunities to learn social skills from typical peers<br>• Children may have similar individualized education plan objectives and needs |
| How many children should I include in my small group? | • Two<br><br>• Three<br><br><br>• Four or more | • Children spend less time waiting<br>• Children have opportunities to observe appropriate social skills<br>• Children have more frequent opportunities for observational learning |
| What kinds of skills can I teach? | • Cognitive/preacademic<br><br><br><br>• Social | • Children learn in a format that may be similar to that used in elementary school classrooms<br>• Children can learn social skills from peers through direct instruction (e.g., teacher prompts turn taking during a game) and observational learning (e.g., child observes peers giving each other praise) |

Table 1 (*continued*)

| Planning Questions | Optional Arrangements or Activities | Advantages |
|---|---|---|
| Should I teach the same, similar, or different skills to each child? | • Same skills (e.g., each child learns to name letters *A*, *B*, and *C*) <br><br> • Similar skills (e.g., Child 1 learns to name letters *A* and *C*, Child 2 learns to name *B* and *D*) <br> • Different skills (e.g., Child 1 learns to name letters *A* and *C*, Child 2 learns to name two words) | • Children do not have opportunity to learn new information by observing peers (not recommended) <br> • Teachers may find it easier to plan instruction <br><br> • Children with different goals can participate in the same activity; exposure to more difficult skills may make learning those skills in the future more efficient |
| Should all children have the same number of chances to respond? | • Same number of opportunities <br> • Different number of opportunities (e.g., more opportunities for child with ASD) | • Children wait the same amount of time; easy to plan <br> • Children who learn more slowly have more chances to learn new information |
| How many chances to respond should I plan in a single activity? | • Fewer trials (e.g., three per skill per child) <br><br> • More trials (e.g., six per skill per child) | • Children may be more engaged and attentive during each activity <br> • Children may require fewer sessions to learn the skill |

ing while increasing the number of skills that each child can learn. On Table 1, a number of questions are presented to guide effective small group instruction. Also shown are potential options and advantages for each.

The first step in small group instruction is getting children's attention. Teachers frequently use a child's name or directions such as "look" or "are you ready?" to get a child to turn toward the task. This may be sufficient to gain children's attention. But in a small group context, teachers can use a wider variety of cues to get children's attention and increase the likelihood they will look in the right direction and pay attention to important aspects of the task. For example, the teacher may have children match to a sample (i.e., match a letter to the same letter before being asked to say it), say the letters before reading a word, trace the letters of a word before being asked to read it, and/or touch the page or card. Even simple motor imitation tasks (e.g., saying "touch your nose" while touching your nose, "give me five" while holding up your hand, and then asking the question) can help cue children to the target. It is also important to think about who you want to respond to attention-getting cues. It may be beneficial to have all children in the group say the letters together before one child is asked to read the word, or only the child who is to answer can be given the cue.

The first decisions regarding group instruction may concern which children to include in the group and what they should be taught. Generally, children who have regular conflicts with one another should not be in the same small group, but different skill levels can be accommodated (Collins, Gast, Ault, & Wolery, 1991). For example, one child could be taught to point to the letter you name while the others are taught to name those letters. Many teachers prefer teaching the same skill to all children (e.g., everyone is learning to name letters). In either case, it makes sense to teach different children different behaviors so they can learn from watching others. For example, when teaching letter names, each child can be taught two letters, different from those his or her group mates are learning. In this example, children would have the chance to learn not just their two letters but also the letters assigned to their group mates.

> *It makes sense to teach different children different behaviors so they can learn from watching others*

Another decision concerns how to disperse directions to each child in the group. You can ask each child one question at a time and then move to the next child. Depending on the child's attention span, you might ask one child three or four questions in a row before moving to the next child. It is easy to ask children to respond by using predictable sequences: First Rachel, then Jose, then Jacob, then Lilly, and then back to Rachel. Another way is to create an unpredictable sequence with children not knowing whose turn will be next. This may help children better pay attention. Asking your questions quickly will help others attend and results in more rapid learning (Carnine, 1976).

Regardless of how questions are provided to each child in the group, teachers should try to keep all children's attention, even when it is not their turn. This increases the chances that children learn what is taught to others. It might be useful to change the number of questions per child turn to keep attention. This could vary by child within your small group. Perhaps some children do not respond well after more than a couple of questions, whereas others could continue for several consecutive trials. Children without disabilities in small groups can often learn quickly with fewer trials than their group mates who have ASD.

Following presentation of the question, the teacher gives the child a chance to respond. Typically, children are asked questions individually and are expected to respond individually. To encourage engagement from other children while one is responding, they might raise their hand if they also know the answer. You should also encourage children to praise their group mates when they answer correctly to encourage children to pay attention to each other. Another possibility is to have all children respond chorally. Although choral responding is a common expectation in large groups and needs to be taught, it does not allow children to learn from observing (Wolery, Ault, Doyle, Gast, & Griffen, 1992). Changing the type of response required may help children to attend for longer periods of time.

Before starting instruction, make a decision about how to respond to children's answers. Generally, you should give reinforcement for correct responses, even those for which children have received help. After they appear to know the behaviors being taught, you can give reinforcement less often (e.g., every other correct answer or on the average of every third correct answer). Some children work well with visual schedules showing the number of responses required before reinforcement. Others may be happy with acknowledgment and verbal praise until the end of the small group. Keep in mind that what is reinforcing is different for each child.

## Recommendations

Teaching in small groups is important and useful for teachers of young children with ASD. Small group instruction is successful when done well and used consistently. However, when done poorly, it is sure to fail. Several practical suggestions for ensuring the success of small group instruction are presented below.

*Variability in how instruction is delivered sets children up for success as they encounter different teaching styles across their time in school.*

First, it is important that small group instruction occur early and often in the education of young children with ASD. Children learn how to learn by being taught by different adults, in different situations, and with a variety of teaching methods. If young children with ASD receive instruction in only one-to-one arrangements, it may be more difficult to learn successfully in small group contexts as they get older. Variability in how instruction is delivered sets children up for success as they encounter different teaching styles across their time in school. Children with ASD may have a hard time paying attention while waiting for their turn, so providing the child with supports (e.g., visual schedules, predictable

routines) while continuing with small group instruction will help the child become more successful in this arrangement.

Our second recommendation is to make small group instruction fun and engaging. One way to ensure these outcomes is to keep small group instruction sessions short and exciting. With 3- and 4-year-old children, 5 to 8 minutes is plenty. As children get older, sessions can last as long as 10 or 12 minutes. Extending it much longer may result in behavior challenges and loss of attention. By watching the behavior of the children in small group activities, you can get a feel for how little or how much support is necessary to ensure that they are engaged and learning what you are teaching. As for making it fun, this depends on your level of excitement and enthusiasm for teaching. The general rule is that children will have no more fun than the teacher is having. Use your knowledge of the children in the group to decide how you can keep the small group exciting and engaging for each child.

Third, we recommend making small group instruction a regular activity occurring at predictable times (e.g., after morning greeting song, after coming in from the playground, after center time) with multiple groups conducted daily as needed. A regular schedule allows children to know what to expect.

Fourth, begin and end each session in a predictable manner so expectations are clear and children know what will come next. When children are comfortable with small group instruction, you can begin to make changes. Keeping small group sessions short and predictable allows you to teach in this arrangement at opportune moments. This could happen at a time when there is a break in instruction, such as at center time, during transitions, or while waiting for other children to arrive. These are great times to pull a small group aside because even if only for a few minutes, you have maximized instructional time in your classroom.

Fifth, pay attention to whether children are learning. Taking data allows you to know how much and what parts of a skill the child has learned (Hojnoski, Gischlar, & Missall, 2009). By creating a data collection system to record responses, you will have information on how each child is doing. You will be able to examine how much the child has learned and the progress they are making as well as any lack of progress. Lack of progress indicates the need for teaching changes, such as simplifying, providing more appropriate prompts, or changing reinforcers. If you see that a child has learned one part of the skill but not another, you can focus more directly on where the child may need more support. Data collection gives you a chance to look backwards and forwards by giving an ongoing account of student progress.

*Lack of progress indicates the need for teaching changes, such as simplifying, providing more appropriate prompts, or changing reinforcers.*

Sixth, consider child engagement during your small group activity. Children must be engaged and paying attention to be able to learn. This is important when considering the extra opportunities for observational learning that are possible in small groups. Encouraging interaction among students during instruction is one way to help this happen. You could have one child praise the other when the child answers correctly. Or you could call the child's attention to another child's behaviors and skills. Setting up routines and facilitating interaction among children will help them to learn while also decreasing the likelihood that problem behaviors will occur. Another way to make sure that children pay attention is to alternate opportunities for learning between children by addressing one skill with one child before switching to the other child, and so on. This prevents extended times when children are not receiving instruction and builds a predictable sequence that the children can understand. You should minimize the time between trials so instruction moves quickly and children stay engaged.

## Summary

We recommend using small group instruction because it provides children with ASD with opportunities to learn in the presence of their peers. Though small group instruction requires careful planning and management, it is an important part of the preschool experience. Beyond the skills that you will teach each child directly, four important additional benefits are noted. It is our position that teachers of children with ASD should use small group direct instruction because it may (1) help peers to perceive children with ASD more positively; (2) help children with ASD to learn from their peers' responses to learning opportunities; (3) teach important skills such as turn taking, waiting, and interacting with peers; and (4) make less restrictive placements possible in later school years. This type of instruction is most successful when teachers incorporate well-planned group work into the classroom in a systematic way. Teachers must be mindful of environmental arrangement, instructional targets, facilitating attention, peer relationships, and reinforcement. High-quality small group instruction will not only lead to increases in use of targeted skills but may also improve general classroom engagement and participation for children with autism.

**Note**

Jennifer Ledford, corresponding author, may be reached by e-mail at jennifer.ledford@vanderbilt.edu.

**References**

Bitterman, A., Daley, T. C., Misra, S., Carlson, E., & Markowitz, J. (2008). A national sample of preschoolers with autism spectrum disorders: Special education services and parent satisfaction. *Journal of Autism and Developmental Disorders, 38,* 1509-1517.

Boutot, E. A. & Bryant, D. P. (2005). Social integration of students with autism in inclusive settings. *Education and Training in Developmental Disabilities, 40,* 14-23.

Carnine, D. W. (1976). Effects of two teacher-presentation rates on on-task behavior, answering correctly, and participation. *Journal of Applied Behavior Analysis, 9,* 199-206.

Collins, B. C., Gast, D. L., Ault, M. J., & Wolery, M. (1991). Small group instruction: Guidelines for teachers of students with moderate to severe handicaps. *Education and Training in Mental Retardation, 26,* 18-32.

Diamond, K. & Huifang, T. (2009). Relations between classroom context, physical disability, and preschool children's inclusion decisions. *Journal of Applied Developmental Psychology, 30,* 75-81.

Hanson, M. J., Horn, E., Sandall, S., Beckman, P., Morgan, M., Marquart, J., et al. (2001). After preschool inclusion: Children's educational pathways over the early school years. *Exceptional Children, 68,* 65-83.

Hojnoski, R. L., Gischlar, K. L., & Missall, K. N. (2009). Improving child outcomes with data-based decision making: Collecting data. *Young Exceptional Children, 12,* 32-44.

Kemp, C. & Carter, M. (2006). Active and passive task related behavior, direction following and the inclusion of children with disabilities. *Education and Training in Developmental Disabilities, 41,* 14-27.

Ledford, J. R., Gast, D. L., Luscre, D., & Ayres, K. (2008). Observational and incidental learning by children with autism during small group instruction. *Journal of Autism and Developmental Disorders, 38,* 86-103.

Odom, S. L., Viztum, J., Wolery, M., Lieber, J., Sandall, S., Hanson, M. J., et al. (2004). Preschool inclusion in the United States: A review of research from an ecological systems perspective. *Journal of Research in Special Education Needs, 4,* 17-49.

Reichow, B. & Wolery, M. (2009). Comprehensive synthesis of early intensive behavioral interventions for young children with autism based on the UCLA Young Autism Project Model. *Journal of Autism and Developmental Disorders, 39,* 23-41.

Wolery, M. (2001). Embedding constant time delay in classroom activities. *Young Exceptional Children Monograph, 3,* 81-90.

Wolery, M., Ault, M. J., Doyle, P. M., Gast, D. L., & Griffen, A. K. (1992). Choral and individual responding during small group instruction: Identification of interactional effects. *Education and Treatment of Children, 15,* 289-309.

Wolfberg, P. J., Zercher, C., Lieber, J., Capell, K., Matias, S., Hanson, M., et al. (1999). "Can I play with you?" Peer culture in inclusive preschool programs. *Journal of the Association for Persons with Severe Handicaps, 24,* 69-84.

# Defining a Role for Parents and Professionals

## Providing Family-Centered Early Intervention for Young Children With Autism Spectrum Disorders

**Marisa J. Salazar, M.Ed.,**
University of Central Florida, Orlando

*Guiermo is a 2½-year-old child suspected of being on the autism spectrum. His parents, Thalia and Carlos, recently enrolled him in early intervention services. An early intervention specialist was scheduled to come to the house once a week to guide the family in supporting Guiermo's development. Initially, they were eager to learn ways to help their son, but they were also apprehensive about the changes that may be necessary and the intensity of therapy their son may require. Once the intervention sessions began, Thalia and Carlos were relieved to learn the ways they were already helping their son and how the smallest changes could make a big impact when interacting with Guiermo. The early intervention specialist was able to support the family without disrupting family routines. Now Thalia and Carlos can enjoy simple family activities such as story time, and Guiermo is able to have fun while learning and growing with his family.*

Children with autism spectrum disorders (ASD) experience pervasive challenges across three core domains of development: communication, social skills, and restricted, stereotyped patterns of behavior (*DSM-IV-TR*; American Psychiatric Association, 2000). Developmental concerns may be apparent from the beginning of life and can be diagnosed as early as 24 months of age (Woods & Wetherby, 2003). Researchers agree that early

*Parents are often given assignments to do between sessions, and multiple professionals may provide conflicting information. . . . [They] are often overwhelmed with tasks assigned to them.*

intervention is essential for children with autism because the most substantial gains are seen with intensive early intervention (Lovaas, 1987; McGee, Daly, & Jacobs, 1994; Strain & Cordisco, 1994; Woods & Wetherby, 2003). There is growing support for the earliest possible intervention that establishes intensity of active engagement time as well as active family involvement (McGee, Morrier, & Daly, 1999; National Research Council, 2001).

Traditional approaches to early intervention have followed a medical model, with professionals serving as experts who work directly with a child. In this model, parents are often given assignments to do between sessions, and multiple professionals may provide conflicting information. In that model, parents of children with ASD are often overwhelmed with the range of tasks assigned to them, and as a result, they may implement little of what is suggested (McBride, Brotherson, Joanning, Whidden, & Demmitt, 1993). Early intervention practices have changed from the child-focused medical model to a family-centered transdisciplinary model (Murray & Mandell, 2006). Active family involvement and individualized supports and services for the child and family are critical features of early intervention (Hurth, Shaw, Izeman, Whaley, & Rogers, 1999). Furthermore, caregivers have identified parent education and support as the most influential and effective service in contributing to their child's progress and development (Hume, Bellini, & Pratt, 2005). Thus, intervention providers and caregivers must explore new roles to effectively meet the complex needs of young children with ASD.

For children with ASD to get the needed intensity of intervention required for successful generalization of acquired skills, it is essential that learning be facilitated throughout the day, not just during therapy sessions (Vismara, Colombi, & Rogers, 2009). With family-centered intervention, the roles of professionals and caregivers are quite different than traditional roles. The main role of the professional is to support caregivers in ways that enable them to enhance learning throughout the child's day (Kashinath, Woods, & Goldstein, 2006; Vismara et al., 2009; Woods & Kashinath, 2007). The parents then interact with the child to facilitate learning in natural contexts, taking advantage of the abundant variety of opportunities that exist throughout everyday family and community routines and activities (Dunst, Hamby, Trivette, Raab, & Bruder, 2000; McWilliam, 1999; Woods & Wetherby, 2003).

Embedding instruction offers children opportunities to practice individualized goals and objectives within the meaningful contexts of existing routines and activities (Pretti-Frontczack & Bricker, 2004). Because instruction is provided in these functional contexts, learning remains interesting and meaningful to both the parent and the child (Woods & Kashinath, 2007). Naturalistic approaches embed instructional oppor-

*Because instruction is provided in these functional contexts, learning remains interesting and meaningful to both the parent and the child.*

tunities within existing routines and are effective in promoting child motivation to learn as well as promoting generalization, maintenance, and spontaneous use of acquired skills (R. Koegel, Camarata, Koegel, Ben-Tall, & Smith, 1998; R. Koegel, Koegel, & Surratt, 1992; McGee, Krantz, & McClannahan, 1985).

Before introducing specific strategies to caregivers, professionals need to take a walk in the family's shoes. Intervention providers must first gather information on typical daily routines and existing learning opportunities that expand beyond basic play routines. Woods and Kashinath (2007) developed a system for categorizing family routines across four categories: (1) play routines such as physical, constructive, and pretend play; (2) caregiver routines such as dressing, hygiene, or food-related routines; (3) preacademic routines such as computer time or reading books; and (4) community and family routines such as family errands or chores. Intervention providers can use these categories to guide open-ended questions about a variety of existing interaction opportunities caregivers already provide throughout the day. Professionals and caregivers collaboratively organize priorities by identifying a few routines across the four categories. Once routines are identified, the intervention provider must observe each routine and recognize the strategies a caregiver may already be using as well as additional opportunities for improved interactions.

## Embedding Learning Opportunities Using Naturalistic Behavioral Strategies

Embedded instruction addresses children's target goals and objectives during child-initiated, routine, or planned activities in a manner that expands, modifies, or is integral to the activity in a meaningful way (Pretti-Frontczack & Bricker, 2004). Through the support and guidance of professionals, caregivers can embed seven naturalistic behavioral strategies within their daily routines (see Table 1). When combined, these naturalistic behavioral strategies are effective in improving communicative, social, and behavioral skills in children with autism (Simpson, 2005). The familiarity of daily routines allows caregivers to predict upcoming learning opportunities and experience confidence when sustaining interactions. When intervention providers focus on family routines, learning activities are more meaningful and consistent with caregiver priorities (Woods & Kashinath, 2007).

Table 1

**Providing Supports in the Natural Environment: An Explanation of Strategies**

| Strategy | Brief Description |
|---|---|
| Contextual support | Gain child's attention, and intervention follows the child's interests. Materials are developmentally appropriate. |
| Environmental arrangements | Changes to physical surroundings that increase learning opportunities: place items out of reach, give small amounts, adjust stimuli. |
| Time delay | Provide additional time for processing and opportunity to initiate. Adult or peer waits quietly with an expectant look. |
| Modeling and requesting imitation | Adult or peer demonstrates a behavior to the child, then helps the child to perform the same behavior. |
| Prompting and fading | Offer support initially and systematically reduce the amount of assistance provided. |
| Natural and direct reinforcement | A consequence that strengthens a behavior. The consequence is natural, contingent, and directly related to the behavior. |
| Interspersing maintenance and acquisition tasks | Varying the difficulty across tasks to increase motivation and frequency of success. |

## Contextual Support

Contextual support involves planning ahead to support the child's attention, motivation, and engagement (Charlop-Christy & Carpenter, 2000; Hancock & Kaiser, 2002; Koegel, Koegel, Harrower, & Carter, 1999). Before beginning a routine or activity, the caregiver gains the child's attention by getting close and face to face. A common obstacle to contextual support is the adult sitting next to the child or with the child in his or her lap. Professionals can guide parents to reposition the child across from the caregiver, emphasizing the importance of establishing face-to-face interactions. Once attention is established, the caregiver follows the child's lead by offering choices and responding to child initiations to maximize motivation and enhance engagement (Pretti-Frontczack & Bricker, 2004). This is done by identifying materials, actions, and objects that are of interest to the child and are at the child's developmental level. Incorporating choices of high interest to the child, such as a favorite toy train or bubbles, helps to keep the child motivated and focused on the activity.

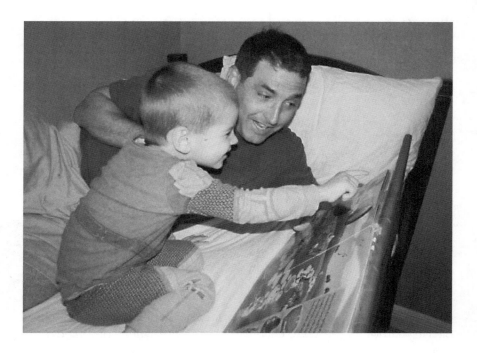

## Environmental Arrangements

Environmental arrangements involve planning ahead and making physical changes to the environment that increase the frequency and type of opportunities for the child to communicate and interact socially (Charlop-Christy & Carpenter, 2000; Hancock & Kaiser, 2002; Koegel et al., 1999; Pretti-Frontczack & Bricker, 2004; Woods & Kashinath, 2007). Limiting access to preferred items by giving only a small amount of a desired item or placing desired items out of reach can encourage social communication. Caregivers can also make changes to the environment by rotating toys. Motivation is increased when old toys are rotated to appear new to the child. Other strategies are to adjust the amount of visual, auditory, or sensory stimuli to enable the child to function without becoming overstimulated. Professionals can help caregivers recognize simple changes within routines that can increase learning opportunities. For example, the next time chips are offered during snack time, rather than give the child a whole bowl of chips, the caregiver can offer as few as one or two and encourage the child to ask for more. This is not to reduce the child's caloric intake but to create a need to communicate before the child is satiated from the first serving. Similarly, if toys are organized within simple reach of the child rather than on high shelves or closed bins, there is no need for the child to interact with the caregiver to gain access to the toys.

## Time Delay

Time delay is used to promote independent responding (Alpert & Kaiser, 1992; Charlop, Schreibman, & Thibodeau, 1985; Woods & Kashinath, 2007). After making an initiation or a request, caregivers use time delay by staying quiet and waiting for a response. This strategy may involve an expectant look, high levels of affect, exaggerated facial expressions, or symbolic gestures such as putting arms up to indicate confusion. Time delay allows additional time for processing informa-tion and gives the child an opportunity to respond spontaneously. Caregivers are often eager to help their child reach a desired response. Many will use a multitude of prompts or repeat themselves in an effort to encourage the child to respond. For example, if a father wants his son to say, "Chips please," he may try to help the child by saying, "What do you want? Use your words. Tell Daddy what you want. Say chips please." Although these are each useful prompts, when combined, they can be overwhelming. Caregivers should be encouraged to simplify their requests, wait quietly, and allow the child a chance to respond independently.

*Time delay allows additional time for processing information and gives the child an opportu-nity to respond spontaneously.*

## Modeling and Requesting Imitation

Modeling and requesting imitation involve demonstrating words, phrases, or gestures about objects and activities the child is interested in and specifically requesting the child to imitate (Alpert & Kaiser, 1992; Koegel et al., 1999; McGee et al., 1999; Woods & Kashinath, 2007). Rather than allowing the child to guess or make frequent mistakes, a direct model of the correct response prevents the child from learning incorrect patterns. Thus, if a child is whining in an effort to be picked up, the caregiver can interrupt the incorrect pattern of whining and model the request, "Up please." By providing this direct model instead of using indirect cues, such as, "Use your words," or, "Ask nicely," the child can immediately respond correctly and receive reinforcement. Models can also be used to support complex tasks or promote appropriate behaviors. For example, when playing dollhouse, the caregiver can begin by modeling, "It is night time, we all have to go to bed," and then laying the doll down in a bed. The caregiver then provides the child with support by motioning to her doll or even guiding her hand to imitate the action and lay her own doll down in a bed.

## Prompting and Fading

The prompting and fading procedure is a way for caregivers to provide assistance when needed and to reduce the level of assistance to promote independence (Koegel et al., 1999). If the child does not respond following time delay, the caregiver can help the child interact or communicate by using extra cues and supports and gradually reducing the level of support to allow the child to be more independent in routines and social interactions. The support can be a verbal model or question, visual representation, physical assistance, or gestural cue. It is important to systematically reduce the level of support provided to limit dependence. Intervention providers can help caregivers develop a plan for both introducing additional supports and for systematically reducing the amount of support provided. Ultimately, the goal is always for the child to be able to perform tasks independently. For example, an intervention provider can guide the caregiver through several steps in the child's transition to eating independently. The caregiver needs support in identifying when to provide help and how to reduce the amount of help that is offered. It may make sense to begin with hand-over-hand physical support with the caregiver holding the child's hand and bringing the utensil to the child's mouth. Following adequate practice, the caregiver may just help the child to scoop the food and then guide the utensil to the child's mouth by supporting the child at the elbow. Next, the caregiver can guide the child's hand without actually touching the child as a final step in the child's independent use of eating utensils.

*It is important to systematically reduce the level of support provided to limit dependence. . . . Ultimately, the goal is for the child to be able to perform tasks independently.*

## Natural and Directly Related Reinforcement

Natural and directly related reinforcement allows the child to understand when he or she has responded correctly as well as to understand the related function of that correct response (Hancock & Kaiser, 2002; Pretti-Frontczack & Bricker, 2004; Schreibman & Koegel, 2005). Caregivers can identify correct responses by offering praise, such as a high five or a smile. However, this should not replace use of natural contingencies. For example, if the child says the word *cookie* as a request, the natural reinforcement would be to give the child a cookie, not a chip or tickles. Such reinforcement should be offered contingent upon a positive attempt or correct response from the child. In other words, if a child is whining because he wants to watch his favorite program on the television, the child should not be allowed to watch the program until he has requested appropriately. The form of the request will depend on the child's developmental level. It may be appropriate for one child to say, "Watch Mickey Mouse Clubhouse please," whereas another child may just make the sign for television or hand the adult a picture of the television to request. As long as the child is making an appropriate attempt at the response, caregivers should provide the child with the desired item or activity. Because the child is gaining access to what is desired, he or she will be more likely to continue to make appropriate attempts in the future.

## Interspersing Maintenance and Acquisition

Interspersing maintenance and acquisition tasks involves varying difficulty levels so that previously mastered activities are infused within new and more challenging tasks (Schreibman & Koegel, 2005). Motivation is maintained as easy tasks or responses are embedded within more difficult or challenging activities. Easier tasks create more opportunities for reinforcement. Varying the degree of difficulty allows a child to experience success while also being challenged. Interspersing difficult or new tasks with relatively easy components limits frustration, creates more opportunities to receive reinforcement, and promotes successful interactions. For example, in a physical play activity such as tickles, a mother may tickle her son whenever he says, "Mommy, tickle me," uses the single word *tickles,* or even uses the sign for more. This allows the game to continue with relative speed and ease, without the child becoming overly challenged.

> *Interspersing maintenance and acquisition tasks involves varying difficulty levels so that previously mastered activities are infused within new and more challenging tasks.*

## Summary

The role of the professional is to guide and support caregivers by modeling use of the strategies within the family's daily routines, providing opportunities for guided practice, and offering feedback. Caregivers should have a variety of opportunities to practice, reflect, and problem solve with the intervention provider's support. Family-centered practices work both to address the core challenges of autism and empower caregivers to enhance parent-child interactions. The familiarity of family routines not only facilitates parents' use of intervention strategies but also aligns intervention with the concerns and priorities of the family (Woods & Kashinath, 2007). Offering caregivers practical strategies and teaching specific skills lead to enhanced child and family functioning, improved overall well-being, and reduced stress (Koegel, Bimbela, & Schreibman, 1996; Tonge et al, 2006).

**Note**
Marisa Salazar may be reached by e-mail at masalaza@mail.ucf.edu.

**References**
Alpert, C. L. & Kaiser, A. P. (1992). Training parents as milieu language teachers. *Journal of Early Intervention, 16*(1), 31-52.
American Psychiatric Association. (2000). *Diagnostic and statistical manual of mental disorders: DSM-IV-TR*. Washington, DC: Author.
Charlop, M. H., Schreibman, L., & Thibodeau, M. G. (1985). Increasing spontaneous verbal responding in autistic children using a time delay procedure. *Journal of Applied Behavior Analysis, 18,* 155-166.
Charlop-Christy, M. H. & Carpenter, M. H. (2000). Modified incidental teaching sessions: A procedure for parents to increase spontaneous speech in their children with autism. *Journal of Positive Behavior Interventions, 2,* 98-112.
Dunst, C. J., Hamby, D., Trivette, C. M., Raab, M., & Bruder, M. B. (2000). Everyday family and community life and children's naturally occurring learning opportunities. *Journal of Early Intervention, 23,* 151-164.
Hancock, T. B. & Kaiser, A. P. (2002). The effects of trainer-implemented enhanced milieu teaching on the social communication of children with autism. *Topics in Early Childhood Special Education, 22,* 39-54.
Hume, K., Bellini, S., & Pratt, C. (2005). The usage of perceived outcomes of early intervention and early childhood programs for young children with autism spectrum disorder. *Topics in Early Childhood Special Education, 25,* 195-207.
Hurth, J., Shaw, E., Izeman, S. G., Whaley, K., & Rogers, S. J. (1999). Areas of agreement about effective practices among programs serving young children with autism spectrum disorders. *Infants and Young Children, 122,* 17-26.
Kashinath, S., Woods, J., & Goldstein, H. (2006). Enhancing generalized teaching strategy use in daily routines by parents of children with autism. *Journal of Speech, Hearing, and Language Research, 49,* 466-485.
Koegel, L. K., Koegel, R. L., Harrower, J. K., & Carter, C. M. (1999). Pivotal response intervention I: Overview of approach. *Journal of the Association for Persons With Severe Handicaps, 24,* 174-185.
Koegel, R., Camarata, S., Koegel, L., Ben-Tall, A., & Smith, A., (1998). Increasing speech intelligibility in children with autism. *Journal of Autism and Developmental Disorders, 28,* 241-251.
Koegel, R., Koegel, L., & Surratt, A. (1992). Language intervention and disruptive behavior in preschool children with autism. *Journal of Autism and Developmental Disorders, 22,* 141-153.
Koegel, R. L., Bimbela, A., & Schreibman, L. (1996). Collateral effects of parent training on family interactions. *Journal of Autism and Developmental Disorders, 26,* 347-359.
Lovaas, O. I. (1987). Behavioral treatment and normal educational and intellectual functioning in young autistic children. *Journal of Consulting and Clinical Psychology, 55,* 3-9.
McBride, S. L., Brotherson, M. J., Joanning, H., Whidden, D. & Demmitt, A. (1993). Implementation of family-centered services: Perceptions of families and professionals. *Journal of Early Intervention, 17,* 414-430.
McGee, G., Daly, T., & Jacobs, H. (1994). The Walden Preschool. In S. Harris & J. J. Handleman (Eds.), *Preschool education programs for children with autism* (pp. 127-162). Austin, TX: Pro-Ed.
McGee, G. G., Krantz, P. J., & McClannahan, L. E. (1985). The facilitative effects of incidental teaching on preposition use by autistic children. *Journal of Applied Behavior Analysis, 18,* 17-31.
McGee, G., Morrier, M., & Daly, T. (1999). An incidental teaching approach to early intervention for toddlers with autism. *Journal of the Association for Persons With Severe Handicaps, 24,* 133-146.
McWilliam, R. A. (1999). Controversial practices: The need for reacculturation of early intervention fields. *Topics in Early Childhood Special Education, 19,* 189-193.
Murray, M. M. & Mandell, C. J. (2006). On-the-job practices of early childhood special education providers trained in family-centered practices. *Journal of Early Intervention, 28,* 125-138.
National Research Council. (2001). *Educating children with autism.* Committee on Educational Interventions for Children with Autism. Division of Behavioral and Social Sciences and Autism. Washington, DC: National Academy Press.
Pretti-Frontczack, K. & Bricker, D. (2004). *An activity-based approach to early intervention* (3rd ed.). Baltimore: Brookes.

Schreibman, L. & Koegel, R. (2005). *Training for parents of children with autism: Pivotal responses, generalization, and individualization of interventions. Psychosocial treatments for child and adolescent disorders: Empirically based strategies for clinical practice* (2nd ed.). Washington, DC: American Psychological Association.

Simpson, R. L. (2005). Evidence-based practices and students with autism spectrum disorders. *Focus on Autism and Other Developmental Disabilities, 20,* 140-149.

Strain, P. & Cordisco, K. (1994). The LEAP Preschool. In S. Harris & J. Handleman (Eds.), *Preschool education programs for children with autism* (pp. 115-126). Austin, TX: Pro- Ed.

Tonge, B., Brereton, A., Kiomall, M., Machkinnon, A., King, N., & Rihehart, N. (2006). Effects on parental mental health of an education and skills training program for parents of young children with autism: A randomized controlled trial. *Journal of the American Academy of Child & Adolescent Psychiatry, 45,* 561-569.

Vismara, L. A., Colombi, C., & Rogers, S. J. (2009). Can one hour per week of therapy lead to lasting changes in young children with autism? *Autism, 13,* 93-115.

Woods, J. J. & Kashinath, S. (2007). Expanding opportunities for social communication into daily routines. *Early Childhood Services, 1,* 137-154.

Woods, J. J. & Wetherby, A. M. (2003). Early identification of and intervention for infants and toddlers who are at risk for autism spectrum disorder. *Language, Speech, and Hearing Services in Schools, 34,* 180-193.

## Appendix

## Identifying Family Routines

| |
|---|
| Describe your family. (Who does your child interact with on a regular basis? List names and relationship to child.) |
| Describe your family's typical routines. (Name the things you do on a daily basis.) |
|    Caregiver routines (food related, dressing, bathing) |
|    Play routines |
|    Preacademic routines (books, TV, computer, coloring, singing) |
|    Community and family routines (chores, errands, outings) |
| How does your child participate in the various routines? |
| Tell me about the interactions you have with your child that are most enjoyable to you. |
| What kinds of interactions does your child enjoy the most? |

# Practical Tips for Educating Young Children With Autism Spectrum Disorders

**Connie Wong, Ph.D.,**
FPG Child Development Institute, University of North Carolina,
Chapel Hill

**Judy Stahlman, Ed.D.,**
Cleveland State University, Cleveland, OH

*"Finally," Allison thought. "I've done it. I finished school. I have my license and a job teaching young children with autism spectrum disorders (ASD)—I'm so excited!" Moments later, as she began thinking more seriously about her job, anxious feelings emerged. "I've learned how to work with young children and families and I've learned about ASD; but how do I really pull this all together?"*

Allison is not alone in her stressful feelings. Many have documented the challenges faced by first-year teachers as they move to their first teaching position (Rosenberg, O'Shea, & O'Shea, 2006; Thompson, 2007). Even veteran teachers can experience uneasiness as they start a new position or begin to work with a group of children who present new challenges. The purpose of this chapter is to provide general and practical tips that can help to ensure quality services for young children with ASD.

## Assessment: Multiple Methods, People, Places, and Domains

*Allison's first step was deciding what to teach. "Where do I begin? I guess I have to start reading those long assessment reports," she thought, "After all, how can I teach if I don't know the child?"*

Before intervention can begin with a young child with ASD, the intervention team needs to review results of assessments so appropriate goals can be written and addressed. However, diagnostic assessments are at times the end result of a long process of testing that may or may not have included the service providers who are actually providing the services.

*It is especially important that the assessment process includes multiple methods such as curriculum-based measures, observations, and family interviews.*

For planning instruction, the service provider goes beyond determining eligibility to review and gather information that will help decide what and how to teach (Odom, this issue). Because many young children with ASD have difficulty generalizing skills to different environments and adapting to new situations, it is especially important that the assessment process includes multiple methods such as curriculum-based measures, observations, and family interviews. Multiple people must also be included to provide meaningful information to guide planning and intervention. This includes family members and experienced professionals with knowledge of typical development and development in ASD as well as in-depth knowledge of specific domains such as speech-language and occupational therapy. Conducting these activities in a closely coordinated process minimizes disruption and anxiety for families and may improve the quality of evaluation findings.

To provide a true picture of the child, assessment should take place in the child's natural environment: the home and any other settings in which the child typically spends time. The assessment should cover multiple domains, with a special focus on social communication and behavior. Service providers must supplement assessments when needed to ensure these criteria are met and that information is current.

## Goals and Outcomes

### Developmentally Appropriate and Functional

*Allison talked to Noah's mother, who reported that Noah is making great progress. Upon request, Noah can count to 10, label colors, and identify shapes. He can even find the trapezoid, and he is only 3 years old. Allison observed him playing at a playground and saw Noah alone, sifting sand through his fingers, while children ran around him laughing, playing, and talking with one another. Maybe Noah should be working on other skills.*

After assessments are completed and reviewed, the next step is to select and write outcomes or goals to guide the intervention. Results of the assessment should highlight potential areas for intervention, but the

Individualized Family Service Plan (IFSP) or Individual Education Plan (IEP) team must identify the most pressing needs to focus on first. What are the most crucial things for the child with ASD to learn? Goals should be developmentally appropriate, functional, and just above the child's level (i.e., within the zone of proximal development) and important to the child's development (Schertz, this issue). Special attention is needed in the core areas of concern for children with ASD: social communication and repetitive behavior or restricted interests. Ultimately, the team must think through why it is important to target each goal or outcome that has been proposed. What is the impact of that goal/outcome in the child's life?

## Observable, Measurable, and Generalizable

*Allison reviewed Noah's current first goal: "In 1 year, upon request, Noah will rote-count to 10 in four out of five assessments over a 2-week period." It's very clear to Allison that to measure Noah's progress on this goal, she just needs to ask him to count to 10 five times and, if he does so correctly at least four of those times, he has met the goal. Noah's second current goal, "In 1 year, Noah will improve his social skills with peers," confuses Allison. She's not sure if this means that he will play with peers, talk to them, make eye contact, or something else.*

Noah's first goal is very straightforward—observable, measurable, and even easily generalized (e.g., count to wait for a turn; count to 10 until time to clean up). But this first goal does not focus on a pressing need. For children with ASD, social communication and/or behavioral goals are usually the most important to address but can be challenging to write in an observable and measurable way (Noonan & McCormick, 2006). This issue is reflected in Noah's second goal. A goal or outcome should clearly define the exact skill and specify exactly how it will be measured. This may include a count of the number of times a child exhibits a skill (frequency) or the length of time a child demonstrates a behavior (duration).

However, there is a fine line between being specific enough and being too specific. For example, the following goal, "During free play in the morning, when told, 'Noah, find a friend to play,' Noah will pick up a toy, walk to another child, and say, 'Play?' while moving the toy toward the other child in four out of five assessments over at least 1 month" suggests that instruction should take place in only one setting and that only one particular method of interacting with his peers is acceptable. Because children with ASD frequently have difficulty transferring learned information to other settings, goals and outcomes should address generalization. Examples of the condition and the behavior should be presented to help define the goal and to ensure that it occurs and is measured across different settings and times and with different people (Noonan & McCormick, 2006). A better way to state Noah's goal for this skill would be, "During a variety of free-play situations, Noah will initiate play or join into another child's play in four out of five assessments over at least 1 month (for example, during free play in the morning, after lunch, on the playground, etc.)."

Finally, when assessing the outcome or goal, consider how data will be collected over time. An objective that asks a child with ASD to engage in a behavior "four out of five times" is ambiguous. Children's behaviors can fluctuate significantly from day to day, and measuring the skill all in one day may not give you a true picture of the child's abilities. Therefore, it is important to assess a child's skills over a period of several weeks.

Table 1 can be adapted as a worksheet to address the required components of IEP goals and to ensure that they are observable, measurable, and generalizable. The worksheet can also be used as a tool to generate IFSP child-focused outcomes and strategies.

## Systematic Instruction

Children with ASD appreciate structure and often show great success learning in small steps. Although every minute of an intervention does not have to be planned, service providers cannot just "wing it." Instruction needs to be thoughtfully planned and systematically delivered (Noonan & McCormick, 2006; Sandall, Hemmeter, Smith, & McLean, 2005), taking into consideration constraints related to individual children, their families, state mandates, and other factors. General intervention guidelines for young children with ASD include embedding instruction in the natural environment, using evidence-based practices, making data-based decisions, and promoting joint engagement.

## Embedding Instruction

*Having learned of its research base, Allison began using discrete trial strategies in a one-on-one setting with Noah but quickly found that he was not generalizing well to other activities. He learned to "show" manipulatives as he takes them out of a box but only to her and only when they are working together at his table, seated across from each other.*

If assessments are thorough and goals thoughtfully selected to promote generalization, embedding instruction within everyday routines and

Table 1
**Worksheet for Planning Intervention Goals/Outcomes**

| Time | Condition | Behavior | Criterion | | Data-Recording Procedures | Importance |
| | | | Independence/ Precision | Frequency | | |
|---|---|---|---|---|---|---|
| When should this be achieved? | What are the environmental opportunities for learning (ante-cedent/stimulus)? Provide examples. | What is the child expected to do? Provide examples. | What will indicate mastery? How well does the child have to perform the behavior? | How often do we expect the child to demonstrate the behavior? | How will this goal be measured? | What is the potential impact of meeting this goal? |
| In 1 year | Everyday routine activities (centers, play time, snack, recess) | Noah will show an object to another person (lift object to approximate face level of peer or adult) | Using at least three different objects within a 20-minute time period/activity | In two out of three different activities assessed over 3 weeks | Frequency count (tallies) of "shows" within each activity | A beginning step to initiating shared experiences with others—an important foundation for verbal social communication |

activities can be accomplished across settings. Because children with ASD often have difficulty with generalization, if instruction takes place in locations and at times in which the skill is most likely to occur naturally, chances increase that the child will incorporate it into everyday routines. This increases the amount of natural practice available; the more opportunities the child with ASD has to practice a skill, the more likely she or he will learn and generalize it. Applying new learning to natural and preferred child activities may also make the process more meaningful for the child and is an important way to promote motivation, active child engagement, and child initiation in learning (Schertz, this issue). Embedding instruction may take extra time and effort initially but becomes more automatic over time.

*Because children with ASD often have difficulty with generalization, if instruction takes place in locations and at times in which the skill is most likely to occur naturally, chances increase that the child will incorporate it into everyday routines.*

A first step in systematically planning to embed instruction is to consider the daily schedule and lesson plans. As illustrated in Table 2, for

Table 2
**Lesson Plan: Embedded Instruction**

| Activity | Students | Child Actions Aligned With General Instructional and IEP Goals |
|---|---|---|
| Group Story:<br>• Read story<br>• Ask "Wh-" questions<br>• Encourage sharing of related personal experiences | All | Answer "Wh-" questions<br>Listen, take turns speaking, follow directions<br>Use four- to five-word sentences |
| | Noah | Show story props to rest of group<br>Use two-word phrases when speaking<br>Count pictures in book |
| | Julia | Initiate comment about book directed to a person |
| | Antonio | On request, point to picture in books<br>Stay in seat with hands to self<br>Imitate vocalizing sounds to label pictures in books |

Table 2 (*continued*)

| Activity | Students | Child Actions Aligned With General Instructional and IEP Goals |
|---|---|---|
| Snack:<br>• Set table<br>• Distribute healthy snack and drinks<br>• Clean up | All | Identify food groups<br>Follow directions<br>Share snacks |
| | Noah | Show snack to other person<br>Use two-word phrases when speaking<br>Count snacks |
| | Julia | Initiate a comment about the snack to another person |
| | Antonio | Point to a snack to request more<br>Stay in seat with hands to self<br>Imitate vocalizing sounds to request for snack |
| Outdoor recess | All | Play with peers<br>Engage in physical activity (run, climb, slide) |
| | Noah | Show toy or any object found on playground to other<br>Use two-word phrases<br>Count by rote to wait for a turn |
| | Julia | Initiate comment about the play activity |
| | Antonio | Imitate vocalizing sounds |
| Center activity<br>• Puzzle center<br>• Children rotated into this center in specific groups | Group 1 (all except Antonio and Group 2) | Independent puzzle time<br>• Practice fine motor skills<br>• Self management: Get, complete, and put away puzzles |
| | Group 2 (Noah, Julia, peer) | Small group instruction<br>• Take turns to put pieces in puzzle (Noah: show puzzle piece to the group)<br>• Talk about picture in puzzles (Noah: two-word phrases; Julia: initiate comments to others) |
| | Antonio | Individual instruction for Antonio: Focused practice of individual goals interspersed with puzzle work |

each group activity, the plan should address where specific instruction for the child will be embedded. To ensure that they benefit from learning that is promoted for the larger group, individual plans should include goals related to the general curriculum as well as individual goals. This approach can facilitate planning for a wide range of performance levels (Dunlap, Strain, & Ostryn, this issue; Pretti-Frontczack & Bricker, 2004).

*Motivated by Noah's progress after embedding instruction for him throughout the everyday classroom routines and activities, Allison did the same for two other children with ASD. Although Julia also showed rapid progress, Antonio seemed to have more difficulty because he is so easily distracted in group settings. Allison wondered if she could combine more intense practice for Antonio within embedded instruction.*

For more complex or challenging goals or for less motivating tasks, some children with ASD may require more individualized and intensive instructional strategies with a partner or in a one-to-one format. One approach is to use task analysis to break the skill into the steps, then to teach one step at a time using repeated practice. Following more intense learning and practice opportunities, teachers can promote generalization to the group environment where further embedded instruction can take place. An example of supplementing embedded instruction with more intensive instruction during a center activity can be found at the bottom of Table 2.

## Start With Evidence-Based Practices

*Allison has mastered embedding instruction on individual goals when appropriate, but how should those skills be targeted? In her university program, she learned that strategies should be research based. After all, if she had a medical condition, she would want doctors to prescribe treatments that have already been proven effective in research studies. But she spends so much time planning and working with children that she doesn't have extra time to find, read, and then try to interpret journal articles. Also, now that she's out of school, it costs money to download research articles.*

Practitioner-oriented reviews of educational practices for children with ASD are emerging. The National Professional Development Center on Autism Spectrum Disorders (2010a) identified 24 evidence-based practices for individuals with ASD along with a series of briefs describing their use in classrooms (http://autismpdc.fpg.unc.edu/content/briefs). These briefs are being converted into Autism Internet Modules by the Ohio Center for

ASD and Low Incidence (National Professional Development Center on Autism Spectrum Disorder, 2010b; http://autismpdc.fpg.unc.edu/content/autism-internet-modules-aim). Additionally, the National Autism Center (2010) published a 2009 report that identifies 11 established treatments, 22 emerging treatments, and 5 unestablished treatments (http://www.nationalautismcenter.org/affiliates/reports.php).

These resources provide a starting point for choosing specific intervention strategies for young children with ASD, although none guarantees success for every child. Research is a lengthy process, and many strategies seen in current practice have not yet been put to the test in research. This is especially true for toddler research in ASD; until recently, toddler-aged children were not identified in large enough numbers for large-scale research studies. In addition, not all strategies have been researched and tested in typical service environments or with children who exhibit the full range of ASD characteristics. Using strategies that have not yet gained evidence of effectiveness may require close monitoring and supplementation with established evidence-based practices.

## Data-Based Decision Making

*Once Allison got all her plans together and implemented them with the intervention team, including the family, she thought she could relax. But from her data, she saw that Noah and Julia were doing well, but Antonio still did not seem to be making much progress. A week later, she saw that Noah was no longer demonstrating the skill he had mastered the previous week. She wondered, "What's going on?"*

After intervention has begun, data collection and ongoing monitoring are required to determine if the intervention is or is not working for the child. Data are bits of information about the child's performance and can be recorded as numbers or as narrative descriptions. The primary value of gathering this information is to guide the intervention; thus, data must be recorded efficiently and regularly and must be put to use (Noonan & McCormick, 2006). After reviewing the data, decisions are needed about whether to give the child additional time and practice to meet the goal, adjust the goal to the next developmental step, reduce the criterion to prevent frustration, change the environment or other antecedents, modify the reinforcements or consequences, or try a different intervention strategy altogether. In this way, service providers can keep up with the child by continually monitoring and targeting higher-level skills as she or he progresses. It is equally important to monitor and modify intervention plans for children who have not shown stable progress on their goals.

## Promote Purposeful Joint Engagement

*With all the planning and embedded instruction, Allison noticed that Noah still spends about half of his free time wandering around, looking off in the distance, and flapping his hands without seeming to be engaged in meaningful activity or interaction. When he is engaged, it is usually with an object and does not seem very purposeful. For example, he likes to lie on the floor and push a toy truck back and forth while looking at the wheels.*

If a child is not purposefully engaged in activities or interactions, the opportunities for learning are dramatically reduced (Iovanne, Dunlap, Huber, & Kincaid, 2003). For young children with ASD, in addition to active engagement, joint engagement is also important (Lawton & Kasari, this issue). This requires periodic checks on whether the child is actively and purposefully engaged with something or somebody and, if so, whether she or he is jointly engaged with objects and with people. An important goal is to increase the amount of time children with ASD are able to engage in activities while shifting their attention between the activity and their interaction partners. If the child is already engaged with either, an important strategy is to follow the child's interest (attentional focus) to promote engagement with another person in reference to object. Thus, when Noah is lying down and pushing his truck,

Allison can lie down beside him and push another toy truck alongside his or playfully block his truck, saying, "Red light!" This sets up an opportunity for Noah to look up and communicate with her (Kaiser, Nietfield, & Roberts, this issue).

> *If a child is not purposefully engaged in activities or interactions, the opportunities for learning are dramatically reduced.*

## Families

*Although Allison felt her relationship with Noah's mother was a partnership, her relationships with Julia's and Antonio's families were different. Julia's mother is a single parent who works full time, so it is challenging to find time to speak with her. She sees Antonio's family fairly often, but they prefer that Allison make the intervention decisions, considering her "the professional."*

### Parents as Partners

Families should be supported as active partners with service providers (Salazar, this issue; Sandall et al., 2005). However, each family is unique. Just as children have various strengths and needs, so do parents. Service providers must be open to collaborating in a way that provides support for the child but that also addresses the expressed needs of families. Families vary in how and to what extent they wish to be involved in intervention planning and implementation (*Parent Voices*, this issue). Responsive professionals do not require caregivers to actively participate; rather, they make it comfortable and easy for

> *Responsive professionals do not require caregivers to actively participate; rather, they make it comfortable and easy for them to do so.*

them to do so by educating them on the importance of their involvement, facilitating conceptual understanding, and supporting parents' competence and confidence with respect to their central role in their child's learning.

### Communication

*Allison recognized the importance of communicating with families, but after writing lengthy daily journal notes, calling families weekly, and conducting monthly home visits, she quickly realized that if she keeps up that pace, it will take too much time away from planning, implementing the intervention, and collecting and reviewing data.*

Productive relationships between professionals and families depend on trust, respect, and communication. Because trust and respect take time to develop, service providers need to begin by establishing an effective communication system with families. Professionals can begin by asking families to identify the most important thing(s) they want to know each day or week about their child and devise a time-efficient system that can be used for parents and teachers to share information with each other. The tone of communications with families should be positive, with an emphasis on what the child is doing well, not only on difficulties experienced. Parents should also be encouraged to share information on successes and issues that arise at home.

Communication can occur using a variety of modalities such as notes, communication books, phone calls, e-mail, and home visits, and these should be customized to accommodate family preferences. Electronic communications are more convenient and accessible for some families than for others. Whatever form these communications take, it is important to respect confidentiality, obtaining and retaining any necessary consent forms.

## Teaming

*Allison now enjoys working with the other professionals on the team; however, it was definitely challenging in the beginning. As a recent graduate, she had a difficult time establishing herself as a qualified professional (she had the feeling that some ignored her and others gave unsolicited advice) and finding time to collaborate with others. But over time, she came to see the value of a cross-disciplinary team because intervention was better integrated and there was less need for pull-out services that removed the child from important opportunities for interaction.*

### Transdisciplinary Approach

In a transdisciplinary model, all members of the team (including the family and paraprofessionals) share as well as learn across disciplines (Noonan & McCormick, 2006). Although Allison was not trained as a speech-language pathologist, with guidance she learned to help Noah practice using two-word phrases and Antonio to vocalize and imitate sounds during story time. Similarly, the occupational therapist incorporated showing and counting with Noah, set up opportunities for Julia to initiate conversations, and elicited vocalizations from Antonio during their classroom interactions.

## Communication

Just like the partnership between parents and professionals, relationships among professionals also depend on trust, respect, and communication. Again, because trust and respect take time to develop, an effective communication system is needed for the team that includes ongoing monitoring and shared

*Time for team communication should be jealously guarded.*

responsibility. This time for team communication should be jealously guarded. Lesson plans with embedded instruction should be developed with full team input. This collaborative approach to planning can result in an integrated and meaningful (rather than disjointed) learning experience for the child.

## Summary

Developing appropriate and functional goals that are observable, measurable, and generalizable and planning and implementing a systematic program of intervention that includes embedding instruction, data-based decision making, using evidence-based practices, and promoting joint engagement—all while teaming with families and other professionals on behalf of young children with ASD—is challenging. This chapter suggests strategies to make these goals manageable.

*Although exhausted from a long day of work, Allison feels exhilarated. Noah's mom had sent an e-mail reporting that at home, Noah had picked up a toy train and showed it to her while making eye contact before playing with it. The general education kindergarten teacher had reported that on the playground, Julia had given a toy cup to a peer and the two girls had a tea party. Finally, Antonio had only one tantrum, and at lunch today, he had looked up at Allison, reached out his hand, and spontaneously said, "Mmm" to request his milk. She was beginning to see that she could make important learning happen for young children with ASD.*

**Note**
    Connie Wong may be reached by e-mail at connie.wong@unc.edu.

## References

Iovanne, R., Dunlap, G., Humber, H., & Kincaid, D. (2003). Effective educational practices for students identified as having autism specturm disorders. *Focus on Autism and Other Developmental Disabilties, 37*, 1264-1271.

Rosenberg, M. S., O'Shea, L. J., & O'Shea, D. J. (2006). *Student teacher to master teacher: A practical guide for educating students with special needs* (4th ed.). Columbus, OH: Merrill.

National Autism Center. (2010). *Overview and results of the National Standards Project.* Retrieved August 3, 2010, from http://www.nationalautismcenter.org/affiliates/reports.php

National Professional Development Center on Autism Spectrum Disorder. (2010a). *Evidence based practice briefs.* Retrieved August 3, 2010, from http://autismpdc.fpg.unc.edu/content/briefs

National Professional Development Center on Autism Spectrum Disorder. (2010b). *Evidence based practices: Autism internet modules (AIM).* Retrieved August 3, 2010, from http://autismpdc.fpg.unc.edu/content/autism-internet-modules-aim

Noonan, M. J. & McCormick, L. (2006). *Young children with disabilities in natural environments: Methods and procedures.* Baltimore: Paul H. Brookes.

Pretti-Frontczack, K., & Bricker, D. (2004). *An activity-based approach to early intervention* (3rd ed.). Baltimore: Brookes.

Sandall, S. R., Hemmeter, M. L., Smith, B. J., & McLean, M. E. (2005). *DEC recommended practices: A comprehensive guide for practical application in early intervention/early childhood special education.* Missoula, MT: Division for Early Childhood (DEC), Council for Exceptional Children.

Thompson, J. G. (2007). *The first-year teacher's survival guide: Ready-to-use strategies, tools and activities for meeting the challenges of each school day* (2nd ed.). San Francisco: Jossey-Bass.

# Resources
## Within Reason

## *Autism Spectrum Disorders Resources*

**Yasemin Turan, Ph.D.,**

**Laura J. Hall, Ph.D.,**
San Diego State University

**Camille Catlett, M.A.**
University of North Carolina-Chapel Hill

The prevalence of children identified with autism spectrum disorders (ASD) has increased dramatically in recent years. According to the National Professional Development Center on Autism Spectrum Disorders, the number of children with ASD served in preschools, elementary, and high schools multiplied nearly 9 times between 1995 and 2007. With these increases comes the companion need to identify high-quality, evidence-based resources, such as those in this column, for use in professional development.

### Evidence-Based Practices

Stansberry-Brusnahan, L., & Collet-Klingenberg, L. (2010). Evidence-based practices for young children with autism spectrum disorders: Guidelines and recommendations from the National Resource Council and National Professional Development Center on Autism Spectrum Disorders. *International Journal of Early Childhood Special Education*, 2(1), 45–56.

The National Research Council has identified goals, areas of need, and basic recommendations for educational programs serving children with ASD. The National Professional Development Center on Autism

Spectrum Disorders has identified evidence-based practices for early childhood and elementary programming. Highlighting the work produced by these two organizations, this article provides professionals with guidance in setting up educational programs that use effective, research-based interventions for young children with ASD in early childhood special education.

http://www.int-jecse.net/V2N1-ARTICLE4.pdf

## Evidence-Based Practice Briefs

The National Professional Development Center on Autism Spectrum Disorders has identified 24 evidence-based practices for children and youth with ASD. For each practice, the Center's Web site offers a brief that provides a general description of the practice and how it can be used with learners with ASD, step-by-step directions for implementation, an implementation checklist, and a list of references that demonstrate that the practice is effective.

http://autismpdc.fpg.unc.edu/content/briefs

## Books

Hall, L. J. (2009). *Autism spectrum disorders: From theory to practice*. Upper Saddle River, NJ: Pearson Education.

This text describes current approaches to increasing the skills of learners with autism organized by theoretical perspective. Descriptions of typical development in the areas of communication and social skills can be used as a guide to selecting goals. Quotes from professionals, parents, and young adults with ASD provide information and insights from multiple perspectives.

Ingersoll, B., & Dvortcsak, A. (2010). *Teaching social communication to children with autism: A practitioner's guide to parent training*. New York: Guilford Press.

Ingersoll, B., & Dvortcsak, A. (2010). *Teaching social communication to children with autism: A manual for parents*. New York: Guilford Press.

This package (two books + DVD) presents a parent training approach that is accessible, evidence based, and highly practical. Grounded in developmental and behavioral research, the *Practitioner's Guide* provides step-by-step guidelines for conducting parent training individually or in groups. It takes proven techniques for promoting the social-communication skills of young children with autism (up to age 6) and breaks them into simple yet effective steps so that parents can learn how to do them. The DVD, for use in the training sessions, features video clips of parents implementing the techniques with their children, as well as PowerPoint slides. The *Practitioner's Guide* also features 30 reproducible handouts and forms. The companion *Manual for Parents* can help parents master the techniques and use them at home with their child during daily routines and activities. Copies of the parent manual are also sold separately.

**Lord, C., & Bishop, S. L. (2010). Autism spectrum disorders: Diagnosis, prevalence, and services for children and families.** *Social Policy Report*, 24(2), 1–21.

A summary of selected recent studies on ASD diagnosis, prevalence, and intervention is provided in this publication. The authors also include strategies for developing social policies to help improve the outcomes and independence of children and adults with ASD.

> http://www.srcd.org/index.php?option=com_docman&task=doc_
> download&gid=930&Itemid= 99999999

**Maurice, C., Green, G., & Luce, S. C. (1996).** *Behavioral intervention for young children with autism: A manual for parents and professionals.* **Austin, TX: Pro-Ed.**

A growing body of research shows that many young children with autism and pervasive developmental disorders can derive significant, lasting, and sometimes dramatic benefits from early intervention based on the principles of applied behavior analysis. This manual, inspired by that research, provides practical information for parents and professionals. It gives the reader concrete information on how to (1) evaluate treatment options and differentiate scientifically validated interventions from fads and "miracle cures"; (2) assess children's skills, needs, and progress objectively and systematically; (3) teach children a wide variety of important skills, ranging from basics such as listening and looking to complex language and social skills; and (4) determine who is competent to deliver and supervise behavioral intervention.

### Topics in Autism Series

Woodbine House has published a number of relevant and practical publications that address different aspects of ASD. Examples of titles in the series include (1) *Reaching Out, Joining In: Teaching Social Skills to Young Children With Autism*, (2) *A Picture's Worth: PECS and Other Visual Communication Strategies in Autism*, and (3) *Teaching Conversation* to *Children With Autism. Activity Schedules for Children with Autism: Teaching Independent Behavior* may be of particular interest to families who are interested in fostering independent engagement with toys and activities at a young age. A list of titles and topics is available at

http://www.woodbinehouse.com/autism-table.asp.

## Web Sites

### Autism Internet Modules

The autism Internet modules were developed to make comprehensive, up-to-date, and usable information on autism accessible and applicable to educators, other professionals, and families who support individuals with ASD. Written by experts from across the United States, modules are currently available to download on reinforcement, self-management, pivotal response training, time delay, and visual supports. Each module has a preassessment and postassessment for the content covered, an introductory video, a description of the topic, and information on how to implement the strategy. Case examples, step-by-step instructions, and the evidence base for the strategy also are included. To access the modules, register for a free account at

http://www.autisminternetmodules.org/.

### Autism Online

Information, books, and other resources on autism in 18 different languages, including Spanish, Chinese, Japanese, and Hebrew, are available at this Web site. A portion of the income from purchases from this site is donated to other autism organizations around the world.

http://www.autismonline.org/index.html

### Autism Society of America

The Web site for this national organization provides current information regarding treatment, education, research, and advocacy in both English and Spanish; links to educational resources; and access to the journal *Autism Advocate*. Members can sign up for a free newsletter. In addition to providing information on autism, there are links to more than 200 local autism society chapters, which have trainings, social events, and excellent support systems.

http://www.autismsociety.org/

### Autism Speaks: ASD Video Glossary

This Web site provides information for parents and professionals on the red flags that indicate a possible diagnosis of autism spectrum disorder. Video examples of the behaviors that could indicate characteristics of the disorder and comparisons to typical child development are included.

http://www.autismspeaks.org/video/glossary.php

## Do2 Learn

Children with autism can benefit from visual cues. This Web site includes ready-to-use picture cards, worksheets, and other educationally relevant activities to purchase. The Web site also offers free picture symbols that can be customized and printed for personal use. In addition, the Web site has a link that specifically addresses the creation and use of visual schedules.

http://www.do2learn.com

## The National Professional Development Center on Autism Spectrum Disorders

The National Professional Development Center on Autism Spectrum Disorders is a multiuniversity center, funded through a cooperative agreement with the U.S. Department of Education, Office of Special Education Programs, to promote the use of evidence-based practices for children and youth with ASD. Available resources include evidence-based practices for children and youth with ASD, Internet modules, and online course content. Information for states on how to partner with the National Professional Development Center is also available at this site.

http://autismpdc.fpg.unc.edu/

## Sandbox Learning

This Web site includes child-monitoring materials to record behavior and to document progress toward meeting individualized education plan (IEP) goals. Communication skills, academics, social skills, fine motor skills, daily living skills, and behavior skills are covered. The materials are available online and in Excel so they can be customized to address each child's IEP goals. A 1-year subscription costs $29.99.

http://www.sandbox-learning.com

## Show Me How to Learn

A free online video modeling library that addresses daily living, language, motor, play, and social skills can be found at this Web site. After signing up, members can watch and share videos and connect with other families and professionals.

http://www.showmehowtolearn.com